A Business Manag
To Agile

A Handbook For Transforming The
Workplace And Job Roles

By Andy S Evans

Edited by L Nisbet

The legal stuff

A Business Managers Guide To Agile
A Handbook For Transforming The Workplace And Job Roles

By Andy.S.Evans

Published by YE&EE Publishing

ISBN 9798799183769

Contents

Introduction

I could just rip into organisations and fill five hundred pages with the foolish things I have seen companies do over the years, but that is not the purpose of this book. That book will have to wait. In this one, I will explain in a straightforward way how Agile can improve your organisation, business, or project. And, why it's pretty certain that some or all of it is coming your way sometime soon. Your work life is about to change, and unfortunately for the slow to adapt, they will be side-lined or even made redundant. There is good reason to think if we introduce systems that work faster (and therefore cheaper) while reducing the paperwork and overhead that businesses are going to be happy. Who won't be happy, are those that delivered the paperwork and processes. If the paperwork and processes no longer exist — then what is their justification to still be there?

When groups of workers organise themselves, who needs the manager? You're not going to be kept around just to sign-off holiday requests. Even for those directly delivering the product you are not immune. If organisations can turn out software in half the time, they only need half the staff. Unless you can see what is happening and embrace it (or look at other opportunities that I will highlight), then you may very well find yourself on the scrap heap.

In this guide, I will walk you through my 25+ years of experience as a Project Manager and look at the impact Agile has on a business. When implementing Agile into a business or working in an Agile environment, it's great for developers and testers to be running around with boards, post-it notes and wonderful new bits of software. However, if the rest of the business is not in tune with what you are doing, all you will manage to do is hit roadblock after roadblock — or as we say in the jargon, blocker after blocker. We are going to peel back the onion of the business and look at how Agile is going to affect the key departments within the business — and most importantly, how to make it a success. Lastly, for those of you already accustomed to working with Agile, I'll share (in my opinion) the best way to deal with obstructionist colleagues, bosses or departments — and navigate the perilous waters of corporate restructuring.

We are going to examine the full business process; from conception, all the way through to the developed and deployed product that needs to be supported in customer care and everything in between. Anything you see in this book has been witnessed by the author in a real-world situation. That means you're going to get the truth and real-world knowledge. Not just nice theoretical wishy-washy statements. I will tell it like it is. I will tell you what you need to do to survive Agile, and even on occasions who you need to fire.

About Me.

My career has mainly been as a freelance contractor; therefore, I have managed to avoid huge parts of office politics and management speak. I always appear to have been at the sharp end of deliveries either hardware or software. My living and my reputation in the industry relies on me getting things done, not being liked. I am not aggressive, but I will tell you the truth and if that hurts, well too bad. I was there to deliver, and office politics or intransigent middle management were not going to stop me. I like evidence-based decision making and want stats to back it up, rather than relying on my gut feelings.

I have worked on insourcing and been the one delivering outsourcing as well as internal deliverers across legal, banking, energy, service management, accountancy, pharma, facilities, education, contact centres and even charities in five continents. At various times in my forty-odd year working life, I have been a logistic analyst, 2nd line support, service desk manager, delivery manager, project manager, programme manager, service delivery manager, scrum master, DevOps manager, product owner and Agile coach and for good measure, I had lots of fun running a software house. Academically I have a degree in Computer Science and another in Economics and Business Studies. On the vocational side, I am qualified in Waterfall, Agile, ITIL and ISO auditing. Budget wise from a few thousand pounds to fourteen million. So, I would say I have a resume that would stand out fairly well to most companies.

I do not want to dwell on myself too much as that is not the point of this book. I would like to give you enough of a taste to ensure you that this has been written from the coal face and not as an academic exercise. I will try and avoid buzz words or management speak and put things in plain simple language. I am not here to help you impress your colleagues with some new acronyms. Rather it is a warning of what is coming your way and a guide to avoid being unemployed. You will have plenty of time to look up a new acronym when you are redundant. If you want to avoid that, then read on.

Welcome To The Wonderful World Of Agile

Why are people interested in Agile? It appears to be a buzzword over the last few years. Mainly in software development, but it is starting to appear in things like marketing and social media. Who knows, maybe one day it may even sneak into the finance department by the back door? The reason companies are interested in Agile, is based on three key outcomes. Firstly, generally, things are done quicker, which usually means cheaper; and most managers like cheaper because cheaper usually means more profit. Secondly, customers get what they want, or at least part of it much quicker than they would have gotten otherwise. Finally, there is the benefit that by working in this way, most organisations reduce defects. The result is the company makes more profit, the customers are happier, and you spend less time running around trying to fix things later.

With these benefits, you are going to really, really have to try hard not to adopt Agile. It becomes incredibly difficult in the boardroom to stand up and put on a convincing case to say, "What I think we should do is increase our time to market, increase our costs and deliver worse customer satisfaction. All those in favour say aye". Pitted against the juggernaut of common sense, you will still find any number of people who will hesitate (if not outright resist) adopting Agile. It's not necessarily that they have a hatred towards Agile, nor are they in any way educated about Agile practices. There are groups of people who just like the status quo. It does not matter what the change is, the problem is change itself. I have a companion book that looks at neuropsychology — in other words, how your brain works — and applies it to business. if you would like a deeper insight into these and other brain business interactions, then you can look up my other book; "How Your Brain Works at Work".

So, let's crack on. We will walk through how businesses normally introduce Agile. Then, let's talk about how they should introduce Agile.

Need To Know Culture Needs To Go!

There are some things in businesses that are regulated by stock markets or other bodies and where there is the potential for fraud either by manipulating the share price or some other factor, then keeping things on a need-to-know basis may be required. However, for many organisations this is a default position, if you are going to replace the Coke machine with Pepsi it is treated as a national security secret. Some organisations management will claim that they cannot let the people know what is going to happen because the unions might complain. If your worker relations are so bad that you feel that if your employees know what you were doing, they would be running up to the boardroom with pitchforks and flaming torches, then maybe you got bigger problems and just possibly you should address those first before trying to adopt Agile. One of the key points of Agile is being open and telling the truth, if something is broken, I want to know now not in six months. Also, we want the whole team to know about it so they can all chip in and try to get it fixed. So, let's look at what normally happens when Agile is introduced, then we will look at how it can be done correctly. Need to know culture needs to go.

Typically, an employee will notice there have been things going on at the head office, senior managers have been in workshops with external consultants and there are post-it notes all over the walls. Next week at the monthly meeting there are rumours about something called Agile being on the agenda. The normal reaction is fear. We do not like change as a species and change mean that we literally must rewire our brains, which is not something we normally volunteer for. What will this mean for my department, for me, for my status and most importantly my money...?

When it does get disclosed then it will be some small pilot team that is pulled together to deliver something which was already pre-planned, pre-budgeted and by the way, has a fixed timescale already set. Now this could be seen as a problem but for most average teams when they get up and running, they can blow the timescales out of the water and that means normally coming under budget. I had one team with a fixed one years' worth of work that we took the team from scratch and delivered in seven months, then had to turn round and ask for more work. The look on that senior manager face was priceless, "no one ever asks for more!".

This is not the ideal way to start. Imagine you were asked by somebody to help coach the local basketball team. When you arrived, you find out that someone else has already selected your team, chosen your tactics and decided to sell your two best players. One of the many thing's organisations get wrong and to be truthful many Agile teams and in particular scrum masters. They forget that Agile isn't just a better method for delivering the software it's also about deciding what software should be built, what gives "bang for buck" and is needed and how can we de-risk it by building it in logical testable chunks.

It is a little bit like assuming robots are cool and everyone else is doing it, so we will automate a production line by sticking in a few robots and it may improve productivity, but are they the right robots, doing the correct tasks. Even more radically should we even be still producing this thing?

It is possible just to start slotting in an Agile team into a pre-existing delivery. You will get some benefits my rough estimation is that you will shave about 25-50% off your delivery time by just putting the raw mechanics of Agile development and testing in place. However, if you get your Agile team in at the beginning from the very start, they will have a much better idea of what you wanted and will be able to deliver it fast which should give a 75-100% increase in delivery. A rough truism that I have noted and measured in real life is that 20% of the effort gets you 80% of the outcomes. We often as organisations spend inordinate amounts of time trying to deliver a utopian package. We have to cover every demographic, we need to make sure that every device ever created on the planet will work, no matter how obscure and unlikely a particular event is we are going to build it into our software and make sure that we test it to bits.

We will cover this in more detail when we talk about projects and the marketing department and this also touches on customer service for which I sadly have to say, having spent some time in the area. It is often seen within organisations regrettably, as an obligation, we have rather than an opportunity to understand our customers. If our customers want to save something as a PDF giving them a chatbot is not going to cut it. Listen to your customer. We can all suffer from the sin of pride and assume that we are so perfect and wonderful that anything that we produce must be the best in the world and there could be no possible reason why any of our customers could find any fault with it. Sometimes it is not that we are delivering something which is of poor quality are badly put together, often where we fail is not delivering what the customer wants or frequently delivering a good product too late. This is a fundamental thing about Agile, we are interested in delivering things that give value to your customers as soon as possible and less valuable things will wait or may even never be delivered.

If there is no bang for buck,

there is no point doing it!

It would be nice if we could think about whether what we propose to produce will be wanted and of the list of things we have on our list which of them are the most important. If I'm going to offer my customers a free download from the latest music charts, I can estimate that I'm going to be targeting a younger audience. Therefore, it is reasonable to assume that these potential users will have a mobile phone. This means it is not unreasonable for me to plan my software development and deployment only onto mobile devices and considering probably 90% of my customers are going to have either standard android or iPhone then that's what I'm going to aim to deliver. I am not going to try and make this a service that is available over a PC and I'm certainly not going to waste my time trying to build this into some kind of telephone or traditional print service.

Now if you want to take the point of view that we've already decided what needs to be delivered and there is a list of features I want you to build for me, then yes you will still get a benefit over traditional methods, but you will get much more, so much more if you have these conversations about what is needed at the beginning. Now let's not kid ourselves, and here I speak from experience, as a waterfall project manager for two decades, they also have these conversations about whether some feature or part of the delivery is a must-have or just some kind of nice to have that could wait till later. By the way, the latter is usually something that has not been funded has no resources or commitment to deliver but leave that aside for the moment. Waterfall project managers have these conversations all the time, the only difference is that they debate this at the end of the project rather than at the beginning. The irony is that waterfall project managers when faced with looming deadlines, overspent budgets sadly have a "Road to Damascus" moment when they become all "Agile" and start talking about the benefits and value of deliveries. Unfortunately, they waste a lot of time and money planning these things often building and testing them and then dumping them. It is like building a house with a garage and leaving out the garage roof and doors because really when we come down to it what you needed was a family house and a garage is just a nice to have. Ok you lose a bit of the garden, and we will tape over the loose wires, so they are safe but as we said we have successfully delivered a house.

I hope by now you may be starting to get an idea that Agile is about delivering value, seeing what the customer wants and delivering that as soon as possible. Other nice to have or could have, will be delivered a little bit later. If you get your team involved at the beginning, they can have these conversations and stop you from wasting time planning to deliver things that are not important

The next thing you want to do to the delivery is to de-risk it. Here is a real-life story working for a large enterprise client. I got web developers to build out the front end and the database guys and gals were building a lovely Oracle backend. Everything was sweetness and light until seven months into the nine-month delivery when somebody noticed that there was a slight problem, the technology version that produced the front end wasn't compatible with what was at the backend and as this was a flagship delivery, (flagship usually means somebody high up in the company has their name associated with this and they don't want to be embarrassed in front of their fellow board members rather than it is really important to customers) but that aside, the fix was to either downgrade the front end which kind of did not work because the point of the change was to deliver the new functionality. Alternatively, you could upgrade the Oracle backend to a new version of Oracle the only problem was that this was in a live system in an environment that could not have downtime, so no pressure then. I got it delivered, Oracle was upgraded and started to talk to the front end then everybody was happy except the finance department. They had to fork out a ton of extra cash for resources to upgrade the enterprise's Oracle estate. Note to all employees, when someone high up says we are going to deliver x by Christmas what is on the line is the date. It can be held together with sticky tape and cost four times more than planned, the key thing is that the important person did not lose face by a delay. You can often use this to extort extra money out of finance departments when you need to. The delivery of this was incredibly expensive because we had to throw a ton of resources at it often out of hours to get it in on time.

What is all this got to do with Agile I hear you cry. The point is that by waiting to the end, to try and put all your components and all your functionality together when something is wrong you are snookered. If I find out in month eight of a nine-month project that there is a serious problem, unless you have all the resources of an enterprise organisation to throw at it, which I had, then you're pretty much-facing disaster. One of the ways you can get around this is to try and break up your delivery into lots of small testable chunks (and I repeat testable, there is no point to give me a bunch of code that I can't test or can't see that it works), I get a login screen week one. Next week I can log in and get to the home screen, Week three I can pick two of the menu items and so on until we are done. By testing bit by bit and preferably testing the connectivity between components then we de-risk the project. We will find problems but if I find out in month one or two, I have a fighting chance to do something about it.

Just think to yourself in real life if, sadly somebody told you that you had stage 4 cancer, there is not a lot you can do about it, but if somebody says because of screening programmes and testing you have stage 1 cancer and here is a list of possible treatments. This is an extreme case, but it highlights when it comes to our health, we want to know early but for some strange reason for many projects we wait to the end to address problems. You do not take all the components of a brand new plane design and bolt them together then say "well let's see if it flies then"

In between delivering all these little chunks of functionality, there may be a point where you've got enough that you can deliver something of use and value to your customer. This is going to have radical consequences for your change management your IT infrastructure and generally the whole service management. The days of the organisation saying we do one major release per year or possibly even two are out the window. We are going to want regular deployments and deliveries because when we have got something useful to our customer could you please explain to me why we would not give it to them. Now imagine yourself walking into a baker and you say I would like a doughnut please and they say I'm very sorry I have a doughnut here, but I can't give it to you because bagels are baking and when they are done we have to bake cupcakes, you will have to wait until the bagels and cupcakes to cook before I can give you the doughnut which you can see in front of you. You would with some justification think that I had gone mad, however, this is often the way that we deliver software and by consequence how we treat our customers.

So now we have some of the guiding principles behind Agile

1. We are going to try and find what our customers value
2. We're going to build the most valuable items first
3. We de-risk it by building it in small chunks and testing it before we move on to the next part.
4. When we have enough that is going to deliver some value for a customer was going to give it to them.
5. To make this happen we are going to create a self-contained team to deliver it.

You may note that we snuck in Item 5 which is teams. To be most effective we want a team to deliver it that is self-contained. This means that the team have the necessary skills, not access to skills via the kindness of some other person but rather the team has all the functions they need to deliver. This typically has a setup that involves analysts', developers and testers and the product owner (whose role is to represent the customer) and of course the scrum master. While this may be a typical set up it is by no means the only set-up. Each team must be built based on what it's got to deliver. If I'm working on building a satellite, I will need communication specialists and all sorts of technical people. Now if my task is to translate a selection of schoolbooks from English into French, I will need a completely different makeup of the team. If the team doesn't have all the skills it needs at a bare minimum it is going to run into blockers or even be derailed completely. There always must be the realism that for various specialist tasks we may have to rely on shared resources but try and keep this to a minimum because it always spells trouble especially if the specialists are not working with or have a good knowledge of Agile.

It is best practice if the team can be co-located, but it is not always necessary, but it does help. I'm sure during the pandemic there have been a lot of people working from home, and they will have found ways of communicating and talking with each other. There are several examples in my own experience where I have had developers in Singapore, testers in Glasgow and customers in Boston. It is possible to deal with teams placed geographically around the world in different time zones, it just makes it harder and if it's harder that's probably slower which is something we want to avoid.

Next, when you have got a good working team you do not wish to destroy it. Ask any coach or manager of a sports team that is winning and ask them whether it would be a good idea to take 25% of the team and put them somewhere else. Generally, the answer would be no. Embracing the concept of teams is going to have quite fundamental changes to the way of thinking for department managers finance and projects, we are going to go into this in greater detail later in the book. For now, it is sufficient to say if you got a team that is working, keep the team together and have this concept of bringing work to the team not the team to the work. The team will be effective if it can make its own decisions and organise itself. This is a big disruptor and gives all kinds of challenges to traditional management structures, again we are going to address these in later chapters. So, buckle up let's go through the wonderful juggernaut called Agile that is about to change the way we work.

The CEO Or President

In some ways you have the easiest job, you indicate a high-level desire to implement Agile and hand it over to your competent teams to deliver. I would expect that you'd want some KPIs (key performance indicators) and you may give some kind of timescale for the delivery. As one of the top people in the organisation one would hope that you have contacts from other businesses and your peers. Typically, it may have been a conversation at the 19th hole of the golf club or a conference, as somebody mentions that "they are beginning Agile" while another CEO says, "yes we did that last year quite successfully" and they turn to you and say, what are you doing with it. A few moments of awkward silence follow and then "Yes we are looking at it as well".

This is not to say it is the "no one got fired for buying IBM" type of conversation but as a CEO if your competitors are getting to market quicker, having happier customers while at the same time lowering their cost base. Then it does not take a genius to figure out that the comfortable lifestyle that I have grown accustomed to is under threat. I have no problem with people trying to protect what they have got because it is how your brain is wired, can't beat nature. The good news for you is that Agile works, time and time again in industry after industry we see faster delivery, happy customers and lower costs.

Now ask yourself if what I am selling is thrown away like a game that you will play for a week or two and then move on to the next thing. For these types of goods, there may not be much return on investment to build in long-life support and continuous improvement. If, however you are in the repeat customer business then maybe you want to think about your product in a longer term than a six-month project timeline. You can still deliver improvements and get that tax right offs using a product-based approach. I will go into more detail on that in the section on the Finance department.

Customers are changing. They expect updates, improvements and fixes constantly. "If Apple can do it why not you", your customers may say. The days of rolling out a new website and letting it fester for three to five years is over. What is this to do with me I detect you thinking "I sell widgets" Whatever your organisation or the product you sell, you are commonly being judged by your software and websites. I can give an example from my own life. I wanted to order some food from a large groceries supplier to be delivered to my home. On my first choice website, I started to notice that things worked fine when you looked through the given lists but if you tried to type bananas it said we don't sell them. Odd I thought and ventured through the menu system and found twenty-three varieties and sizes of bananas. Giving up in frustration I went to a competitor's website and found bananas easily by a search, they got my order and every one since.

Amazon is no longer a bookstore, it is the website, the mobile app and Alexa. Without its technology and that technology working, there is no business. I have seen in my time disaster recovery having to be put in for real and let me assure you there are very few large organisations out there that can cope without their functioning IT and supporting software. If you went into the office and they had taken away everyone's PC, how long would it be before your business processes were disrupted? Would you feel confident that you would even get paid? Even if you are not working directly with the Agile development teams you and your work life are tied at the hip to what they produce so you better hope they make good quality working software, or your days are numbered.

So, let me ask you if you have a plan to sell a product for the next say five years, why do you not put in support of that product and the system that support it. You can either have an Agile product team for five years improving and updating your system all the time or hire support staff to fix bugs, write apology letters to your customers and have the sales team issue credit notes and refunds. Roundabout year three or four pay for marketing consultants to tell you that your systems are getting dated and seen as old fashioned compared to competitors, initiate a project team to start from the ground floor and reanalyse the product and its functions and come up with some new ways it could be improved. Kick in the finance department to push wooden dollars around and finally and belatedly give your customers what they have been asking for, for three years. All the while driving your sales teams to make up for lost revenue to your competitors and explain to your shareholder why this revamp of the software is needed and why they need to pay for it. Take this recipe and leave to settle in a data centre for three to four years and repeat.

It costs a lot of money to start up a project, I should know I have spent enough of your money over the years. (By the way thanks for the two houses, ten cars and a bar that you paid me for as my small contribution to your projects). You would not build a factory and produce 100,000 units, mothball it, then build a new factory for the next 100,000, but we do this with Software. So, we expect that in a digital age where the next technology change was yesterday that we can throw a pile of money at some software or web offering and that is the job done. Nothing is going to change; the marketplace is static, and our competition sits on their hands admiring the view out of the window of their corner office. Why not for less money, get a team together that is going to look after and care for this product for the full five years. The change will be gradual and steady, each pain point in the process removed one at a time and it will not stop there as user demand for face or voice recognition, or the latest phone or watch device comes along you can adapt your products software offering.

Product-based development is cheaper, if I know I need two developers and a tester for three of your five years is the same price as contractors for one year. Then as we have staff on hand that also pick up the support costs for the product long term support is not required. Finally, 15-25% of the entire cost of the project is eaten up with project costs. Here is some interesting news if you have a product team you don't need a project. Bingo we are often looking at negative cost to the organisation to have a product team for five years compared to contractors for one to two years running a project. If I was taking out a warranty on a car and I got offered one year or five at the same price, I know which one I would choose. Added to that all product knowledge does not walk out the door at the end of year one.

There are huge swathes of your money going on managing projects that you do not need. No projects office, no hordes of cost accountants in finance departments to produce project reports spend because there are no projects, just products. It is typical for project costs to be 10-25% of the cost of a project. That is a quarter of your money being spent on monitoring that you are spending your money. If a bank or an investment company wanted a quarter to look after our money there would be riots in the street, but we have built up an industry that is based on we need to spend money to ensure we don't overspend.

No one cares if you come in under budget, so the sole purpose is that we are monitoring for the overspend. Now, I will occasionally have a little bet on a horse race and if someone said to me that projects tend to overspend in the range of 5-17%, so my cure for that is to spend 10-25% of your money. I would say that was a bad bet. Even the ones that do blow the budget are seldom if ever dumped. We get the "well we have come this far, we may as well finish". So, the whole apparatus that we have invented just manages the handout more cash, with change controls, i.e. I want more money. With a product team, you have a fixed number of resources. This means a fixed cost. You cannot go over budget. Therefore, no need for a project office, financial control or financial reporting.

When we tell people, exactly what to do, when they can do it and they need to ask express permission to deviate in any way from our commands, you may even go further stating when people can eat and go to the bathroom. Sounds like corporate heaven, but there is a flaw, when we do that, it is called prison and people do not like a prison, so they rebel and resist. No worries we can impose a group of prison guards, oh sorry managers, to monitor and report on activities. To reduce the possible disruptive elements getting in or described as blending in with our corporate culture as it is sometimes referred to. We want docile and obedient drones. This means we need to invent human resource management to ensure that we get this type of corporate culture to approve personnel. We can add further restrictions, even though you the CEO have said get this done by Easter or we are all out of a job, no one is allowed to lift a finger until they have been issued with a budget code to enact what you say. You can demand anything you like as the CEO it will not happen without a budget code. This means the clerk who issues the budget codes on a lowly salary is more powerful than the CEO and the board.

Especially in office base jobs when I look at the ratio of finance staff, human resources, project office and managers of all shapes and sizes (by the way the only time most people notice that the manager is not there is when they need authorisation for something, back to those old budgets again). I coined the phrase the doers and the watchers and it is not uncommon that 30% of your business is engaged in some form of watching the rest of the business. Money well spent I am sure you will agree. Maybe there is something here that we could change.

As the CEO of the organisation if you are going to implement change, please be aware that change will mean doing things differently. I know this sounds like a statement of the bleeding obvious but in twenty years of project management and a further ten in Agile you would not believe the number of well-meaning conversations I have had, where people tell me

"This is how we do things" and I have to interject "that is how you used to do things". It is utterly bewildering to me the number of people in organisations that when confronted with change assume that every process and procedure they have will remain in place, inviolate until there is a vote in the house of representatives by a two-thirds majority and ratified by the Pope before making a change. When I am hired to implement change, I am confronted with an attitude that they would like me to change my change to fit in with their existing ways of doing things.

For some of your department heads and managers, they will see this as a potential risk and give all kinds of excuses about why while it all sounds wonderful it's just not the right time at the moment. If you can substantially change the way that you do software within your organisation with the benefits listed above of happier customers quicker development and saving money, then I'm afraid that you should also reply with your HR department that you may need to do a little bit of restructuring of some of your functions because there are no longer going to be needed or going to need to be doing something different. I can conservatively estimate that 15% of the staff that are not front line i.e., generally classed as some sort of admin function can be pruned because the bits of paper, they used to push around is not needed anymore.

I've worked with CEOs, vice presidents & directors and had conversations with them along the lines of "well we tried to bring in Agile and it didn't quite work". I tend to ask them what they are doing that makes them completely different from every other organisation in the universe and normally I don't get an answer to that. Unless someone can give me some really good compelling reason why the structure of the organisation is so absolutely unique that Agile cannot be deployed then I start looking for other factors. It could be the people we got in to do it were not competent, this is a risk that you take in anything you buy and applies to consultancies as much as it applies to takeaway pizza places, they don't always deliver what they advertise. The next most common thing I start to look at is the structure of the organisation, to be honest with you that is the most likely place to be the problem. I hear stories like "Oh yes we got a team together and he started to develop the Agile and then we had another project kicking off, so we took half the team away to work on the new project. Then we backfilled with freelance contractors but one of them left because we only offered them a three-month contract. Then you go and talk to some of the people in the team and they tell you tales about not being able to deliver software rapidly because the current change management and deployment process only deploys twice a year. They were asked to fill in forms and do audits and checks which failed because the audits and checks were designed for a waterfall. "Show me your project plan", answer "we don't have one this is Agile, we have a prioritised backlog", response "failed compliance checks, no project plan in place" as an example.

The responsibility of the CEO who wants to implement Agile in their organisation is not only to kickstart the implementation but to make it clear to everyone in the organisation, that because we are implementing change that means every policy, procedure work practice and statement of work that we have, may also need to be changed or even removed entirely. There is no point implementing a fully automated robotic production line and then asking, "what time do we shut down the robots for their afternoon coffee break because we always have an afternoon coffee break". This may sound a little bit absurd, but it is no less absurd than some of the comments I've heard when implementing projects. Please let all the organisations know that change means change. Potentially the knowledge that at least 15% will not be there next year and we are looking for the ones that can be flexible enough to embrace change, may just be enough of an incentive to get them to pay due attention. This is not a joke you will no longer need a lot of people to do admin functions. If I can develop software in half the time, I can choose to reduce the staff in half or deliver twice as much. We implement five-year plans with growth projections of 3-5% per year.

Department budgets are challenged to reduce costs by 5% over three years. These figures are peanuts compared to 50-200% cost savings on software development. Not to mention the competitive advantage you have of being first to market. Add into this mix that you do not need at least15% of your admin staff and we are starting to talk about real radical changes.

The Department Heads

Here I am going to use the term department head loosely. All I mean by this is somebody who manages people to deliver a function or a service either internal to the business or the customers. I am not wanting to get into the minutiae of whether you are managing two people or twenty thousand some basic principles of management apply regardless of the numbers. I will try and give examples of big and small organisations and hopefully, some of them will relate to your situation. So, if I was too dumb it down a bit you would see that you manage people who do stuff.

Traditionally department heads focus on budgets. I can hear in my head any number of readers saying to themselves I'm not focused on budgets we are telesales teams, ambulance drivers or a pizza deliveries company, it doesn't matter what you're doing you are restricted and controlled by the budgets you have. We define the scope of what we are being asked to deliver, we then state what resources we feel we need in terms of people, technology and equipment to deliver and then put a request in usually annually for a budget to deliver the said things. The normal practice is that we will ask for much more than we need in the hope that when it goes through the finance department and gets pared down, we will get something approximately to what we were looking for, but as every other department head is playing the same game we compete. Somewhere somebody is going to decide our priorities and not everything on our list is going to get approved. Just like the nine-year-old child, we may face a bit of a disappointment when we do not have that new bicycle, VR headset, the latest trainers, Xbox, PS5 and a puppy that we had asked Santa for.

As a department head, you may have other parts of the organisation asking you to approve budgets and they will equally be aiming for the stars and the moon and have a resource list that could form a small army. This merry-go-round usually goes for two or three months until the budgets are formalised in which case you do not manage scope and resources you are given a budget which states what resources you can have; the scope was curtailed to suit the budget, which in turn means the scope of functions and services which you can offer are directly dictated by the budget you are allocated. Like a general you have been handed your troops, they are your people, you had to fight hard for them and get those resources allocated now that you have, we can move forward to delivering the first-quarter goals. Repeat this exercise every nine to twelve months until you retire.

There are a few fundamental flaws with this process, namely not everything fits into a neat twelve-month cycle. Any number of projects are going to run for longer than a year and while we make expenditure models and resource plans and sit there with our project plans, we know that reality is going to strike at some point and these plans are going to go out of the window along with the budgets. Here is one of my favourite studies. A group of senior managers were asked to make predictions about whether particular projects were going to be on time and budget. Their predictions proved to be fairly accurate for up to three months. They could reasonably assess the risks and possible impact to the projects, beyond that it wasn't so good. Now anybody who does betting will be able to tell you that picking the odds for one horse to win a race is hard enough, but if you wish to see who's going to win multiple consecutive races it is an order of magnitude harder, and this is for events that are statistically separate and not connected.

The problem mathematically with projects is we have interconnected risks that cascade like falling dominos. We can probably estimate what the impact of one thing going wrong is and how it can affect the project overall. For example, if you are building a house and bad weather delays us laying the foundations by two weeks, it is relatively easy for us to move all the subsequent tasks to the right by two weeks. Reality is not usually that simple, the company that was to build the brick wall on top of the foundations may be booked in two weeks because they thought that they would have the job completed by then, so they inform you at the next window of opportunity they have is in one month and equally the joiners inform you that they have availability but as we're coming up to a holiday period, they may not be able to supply a full squad and some of the staff will be going home for the holidays. Some suppliers will be able to delay the deliveries while others are already in transit and will arrive at the site, which will mean that we will need to create some temporary storage space and pull resources from other areas of the job. Some staff are working at fixed cost others are day rate, so these delays are going to affect the budget. This will in turn require us to raise a change control for additional funding. We may be able to potentially lower some of the costs if we go for double glazed windows rather than triple glazed but there is an eight week led time from the supplier.

These are not too unrealistic for the types of things that happen in projects or departmental initiatives. Often one delay has a knock-on effect on other teams or deliveries. As the impact cascades throughout the project, it becomes more and more difficult to predict the outcomes. There are some fiendishly difficult mathematics where you can work out the probabilities of consequential risks but even if you have a Master's degree in mathematics and you do these calculations all you're left with is a probability of your project finishing on time and budget. If you calculate that you have a 63% chance of your project finishing on time how is that going to help you make your decision? When you're 98% certain or your probabilities drop down to 5% of success then at these extreme edges, it's very easy to make decisions. When you're in the region 40 to 70% it is kind of down to gut feeling rather than any kind of mathematical formula. Because of this cascading complexity, we find that predictions beyond 90 days can be wildly out. The example we gave above about the house build only looked ahead about two months but honestly go through our project deliveries they'll be something else in one month and yet another the following month.

Statistically, real-world evidence, experience and theoretical studies all tell us that when we go past 90 days for our predictions we may as well ask chimpanzees to roll a dice, we have a statistical probability the dice will be as accurate as our expert opinions. Therefore, all this financial planning and looking for the year ahead and what we're going to do in quarter three and quarter four is quite honestly a waste of time. The impacts of what happens in quarter one are going to so substantially affect what is available for us to do in quarter two that these plans are probably 50/50 and by the time we expand that out to quarter four, we will get some items that are just impossible to complete, or we have run out of budget. In terms of business efficiency, this appears to be a complete waste of time, energy and most importantly money. It is compounded by any number of KPIs and reporting that we tried to do about the deliveries and the financial spending because we feel we need to justify the budgets we have been given. Large amounts of management time and project staff time is taken up with meetings explaining to people because of the bad weather we were delayed and because of the delay in laying the foundations the bricklayers needed to put their stuff back which affected the joiners and as a result, we had to try to cut costs, so we ordered different types of windows. There was a lead time for that and so on and so on. We spend time analysing, assessing, changing our project and financial plans, followed up with the change control process. All the while burning through time and money. This partially explains some of the reasons why we spend 10 to 25% of our project budget on managing the project.

Have you ever been asked to hand back money if you did not deliver something that was listed in your budget proposal, or is it the case that there is a long line of excuses that explain why the SQL upgrade did not happen or that improvement program only delivered a 1% return rather than the predicted 12%? If you were to be radical about it you could introduce a quarterly budget to get you started and like stage gates in projects, you would need to show progress to get the next quarters money. At least this way people would be focused on delivery, get their backlog and start delivering it. See Agile in areas other than software. If we know that we are not going to get the SQL upgrade done in this year's budget, why are we allowed to hold on to that budget? Why not give it to someone that can deliver.

Now I will give one shout out to the project managers. From my experience what distinguishes a good project manager from a poor project manager is the ability to think on your feet and manage the inevitable changes which are going to come along. Where you can earn your spurs is in dealing with the chaos which is caused by the two-week delay in the foundations and organising all the other teams and suppliers to get yourself back into some kind of order. When you are interviewing a project manager ask about what they did when things go wrong. Don't worry about processes and procedure type questions, when the pooh hits the fan, I want someone that can fix it, not file a report on the expected spread and potential smell hazards.

It is also possible that as the department head you may be the consumer of software services. The service desk manager may need some tweaks to the front screen of the helpdesk software. The HR department may want some forms to put online, or the finance department may want to automate a workflow.

Typically, you are asked to document in as much detail as you can, exactly the changes that you wish to implement. There may be an additional period of investigation because surprisingly even though a particular bit of software may have been in support for many years the documentation may not be up to date, or the working knowledge may have left the organisation some time ago. Therefore, you need to pay to have someone reinvent the wheel and analyse how your bit of software works under the hood. I do realise under best IT practises whole support processes and configuration are fully documented, just like all politicians a scrupulously honest and have only the best interests of their constituents at heart. That is to say from forty years of experience there is often not the level of documentation and knowledge that in theory should be there.

As the department head, you spend a month or two of your resource's time, trying to explain what the problem is and what the fixes you would like to see. The team that is going to deliver it get all this written up by a third party, who will then attempt to replicate what you have told them and explain it to some developers. They will in turn try their best to interpret what they've been told and come up with some estimate of how long it will take to deliver, if you're lucky at this point there will be some afterthought is put into possibly this thing may need testing and we better lump on a little bit extra for testing. This whole process transforms into what is effectively a quote from the IT department to do some work for you. If you have one of those things called the budget, you may agree to the cost. This will kick off a project, the project office, finance, and IT get together and form a project pulling together people who may be able to deliver it, loosely associated with the technical skills to deliver it but more commonly it is who is about to finish up a project and is available. This can take from a month to six months to start work. Typically, this will be delivered in a waterfall fashion, and it'll be a further six months before you get to see what they hope is a final product. We have to hope but nothing happens in this interval of a year that makes the requested change obsolete. We also have to hope that the original requester can remember what it was they wanted a year ago. If when you see what is presented is not to your liking, then it's a little bit late in the process to make major changes. You may insist on this, but any alterations will likely come with an associated price tag which you're paying out of your budget.

Let's do a thought experiment and assume that we have a fully Agile environment. In this world, we will have a product team associated with our application. When we want to change some of the processes, we have a team that knows how the application works because they are the people that support it, they make changes to it and deliver any project work. Instead of you telling somebody else (usually an analyst) what you want and that person telling the development manager what they think you want, who in turn translates for the developers what they think the analyst thinks you think. In Agile the group of honest testers and developers who are going to deliver this come and speak to you directly. They break down what you want to deliver into small chunks of functionality, ask you what is the most important, and then start building that first. In this way, within two to three months you may get your data captured, a month later it will automate some of the error handling and checking. Two months later you get the backend processing and in the final month six, you get the reporting that you wanted. Even as the first part is being built you will regularly be invited to view progress. If there's anything you think needs changed or you suddenly remember that you've forgotten, that can be incorporated into the build and in a couple of weeks, you'll be asked to view it again.

The processes I have described here are very typical, almost average for the Agile approach. One of the huge areas where Agile scores are the assumption that things are going to change as we go through the process, therefore there is no advantage in going through a lengthy and costly analysis stage where we document everything in excruciating detail before we start. Partly because no matter how good your prose it's not as good as talking to somebody and that written document is out of date as soon as it lands on the printer.

This theoretical stuff aside it is clear to the department head, one method is going to deliver something to me in a year and I have to hope it still meets all the requirements I initially set out and that nothing has intervened in the meantime either from our competitors, external legislation or our internal process, that could make some or all of the delivery useless. Alternatively Agile is going to start taking away my pain in little chunks. I say pain because nobody goes into making a change to software unless there's some compelling event, this could be equated to pain. There's something we're doing badly or there's something we need to do that we can't. My pain is going to be taken away a little bit at a time but I'm going to have a fully working product in six months and because they have not had a lengthy upfront loading it gets delivered to me quicker and cheaper. I also have the advantage but within common sense limits, I can make reasonable requests to make alterations to the look feel and functionality of the software while it's still in the process of getting developed. Most Department heads given the option of faster and cheaper will choose faster and cheaper.

There is often a disincentive for Government organisations to deliver cheaper. Within any number of government departments around the world if you do not spend your full allocation of budget in a particular timeframe then you will lose it. You may even be told off. Central government planners will argue that if they had known that you were going to underspend, they may have been able to reallocate that money to some other worthy cause like emergency ambulance systems or sponsoring an art gallery. I faced exactly this problem when delivering for one government client using Agile. I was sure that the client would be happy that we had delivered seven months early and 30% under budget. In my naivety I was not prepared for the level of anxiety this was going to give my client. I had suggested that as we have a budget and time that potentially there may be some other work that we could pick up. This I was informed would not be possible because any work undertaken must be sanctioned by a central authority and for us to go back and request approval to undertake additional work would indicate to the central authority that they could not trust our planning estimates originally submitted half a year ago. There is only so much you can do as an individual project manager or Agile coach. If the organisation you are working for decides to work irrationally, there is not much you can do about it. Sometimes I describe this in terms of, if the customer asked me to go to the roof and throw brand-new laptops into the car park below, provided we have implemented the necessary health and safety prerequisites I will organise it to be done. After all, it is your money.

The Project Manager

If you are a typical waterfall project manager, you will have your plans in Microsoft Project or some other hybrid clone. They may be comforting but stop doing it. As we highlighted in the department manager you can only reasonably predict ninety days. After that the risk impact and combination of risk after risk are so great you can roll dice and get an equally statistically valid answer.

Now let me prove this to you by asking a few simple questions. Where will you be in exactly one hour, there's a good chance you will be able to tell me with a reasonable level of accuracy with an answer like "I'm going to be in the qualifications review meeting". When I extend this out and say to you where are you going to be in thirty-seven days and where are you going to be having lunch, this starts to get a lot trickier, because we do not normally plan our lives that far ahead unless it's a major event like a wedding or going on holiday. In the normal run of the mill, we plan for today and tomorrow and loosely plan in events like the dentists as a flag in our diary that we will need to workaround.

When we start asking things like, "where are you going to be having lunch in thirty-seven days", you start getting a kickback from people saying, "how am I supposed to know where I am going for lunch that far ahead or even if I am going to have lunch that day". Now when I finally ask you where you are going to be in one hundred and twenty days at 2:15 in the afternoon, you're probably going to dismiss me by saying "that's a stupid or crazy question to ask" because how are you supposed to know exactly where you are going to be at 2:15 in one hundred and twenty days. What an absurd question to ask. Interestingly we have no problem predicting these future dates and what other people are going to be doing exactly at that time. For example, we can tell that Jean in one hundred and twenty days at 2:15 is going to be working 100% on the project go-live communications. The reason we know this for certainty is that we have a little blue line on a Gantt chart that tells us so and if it is on a Gantt chart it must be true.

General Gantt, by the way, was an American during World War I and he reckoned that the problem wasn't with the morale of the fighting troops it was a logistical problem. We would break through the enemy lines and run out of supplies and the breakthrough would halt. So, to sort this problem all, he had to do was to make sure that all equipment and resources that were needed were in place. The guns, the horses to pull the guns and enough hay for the horses. Bandages for the wounded, stretchers, the appropriate number of stretcher-bearers and so on until the entire battle was meticulously resourced and planned. This would ensure victory. While it was a noble effort to try and organise the logistics of the army unfortunately as the war dragged on for a further two years this did not have the desired effect and was, in fact, a failure.

As an interesting quirk of the human mind, we will hold onto a fantasy even when we know that it is not borne out by reality rather than accept uncertainty. Therefore, we get great comfort from our project plans and schedules which show that we have enough horses and sufficient bandages for the wounded. All the while knowing in our heart of hearts that what we are putting down on paper today is not going to be a reality in nine months. One of the interesting intellectual challenges to present to any planner from the example above is to ask can you confirm that Jean will still be working for us in one hundred and twenty days or for that matter will she still be alive. The basic premise is you stop planning more than three months in anything other than big picture desires. The complexities of delivery are so large that ninety days should be a limit.

This poses an interesting question when we are going to plan work. A traditional method is to get the project pool of internal and external resources together and kick off the project. If you read the section above about the CEO you will see there are some operational issues with this. In the modern world, the economy and our customers do not stand still and especially our competition. Building something to deliver in a year and hoping it is still going to be relevant is a dangerous assumption to make in a modern economy. It is also not very efficient burning through 10 to 25% of your cash resources to monitor it. In most organisations, items taking a couple of weeks to a couple of months are picked up by the Business-as-Usual support teams. This could include minor upgrades of versions, a few new pages to a website or introducing new IT tools into the estate. When we go beyond these time scales, we instigate a project.

To reduce risk, it was thought best to spend up to 25% of the cost on the analysis and design stages. Going from rough orders of magnitude to high-level estimates and usually low-level estimates. How can we say how much it will cost if we do not know the exact specification of the delivery? There is a law of diminishing return at play here, where each round of refining the specification, design and associated changes has a cost for the resources to carry out the investigation. Eventually, that cost will be more than we will potentially save. This means that we never get the full and exact scope and cost. If you read my other book How your brain works at work, I explain how this method of estimating is normally in the range of 50-200% out. Now I hear you cry "I don't have any projects that were 200% over budget" and that is true because when you start to run out of budget you cut quality and scope, testing is reduced, the nice to haves are dumped and we often go into production with known bugs and broken workflows with "manual workarounds" which we hope are not so serious that the whole thing will crash and burn.

Now I am old enough to remember the days before we had formal project management standards like MSP or Prince2. Back in the eighties, there were several spectacular failures. One was in the National Health Service and the other in the London Stock Exchange. They both thought that computerisation of the processes was the way forward and kicked off projects. What both projects suffered from was a lack of structure and soon the scope was expanding and every passing good idea or suggestion that someone had at a meeting was added to the scope regardless of what value the feature had. Effectively everything was a must-have. As the scope increased so did the complexity and the cost. In both cases they had been running for years, blown large amounts of money were still at the analysis stage and were eventually cancelled as failures.

To prevent these things from happening again methods like Prince2 were developed to specifically restrict scope creep by introducing processes that required, analysis, costing and approval of all changes. We would go into more depth in understanding what was there and what we wanted to deliver and record these in requirements documents. Stage gates could be applied to allow us to check progress before ploughing more money into the project. As the computer industry was in its infancy at the time, very few organisations had the internal resources to deliver the project and the contracts market had not developed enough to have a pool of people you could call in. For these large projects, it required bringing in outsourced partners. When we had third parties the deliverables needed to be put in a contract and this restricted the ability to adapt throughout the project because it required not only the agreement of the teams delivering but also legal contract variations.

There is an interesting study from history that highlights the issue with an unintended consequence. The Indian government wanted to increase the amount of productive land for agriculture. One of the problems was that there was unused land available, but these areas had large numbers of cobras. Naturally, farmers did not want to die so they avoided using these areas. The Government hit on a scheme to put a bounty for every dead cobra that was delivered to the local agricultural board office. Sure enough, people started to turn up with dead cobras. The next problem they faced was they were paying out too much money and there appeared to be more cobras being handed in than could normally be expected to be found in the wild. When this was investigated, they found that farmers incentivised by the payments had turned to rear cobras for the bounty. As this was not the intended result the government stopped the bounty. The farmers now did not need all the captive cobras then released them into the wild. The result was the government had spent a lot of money and now had more cobras in the wild than when they had started our unintended consequence.

When we look at unintended consequences in the software market, we see the following. The company supplying the software was restricted by the terms of the contract. If an eagle-eyed developer or analyst noticed that requirement 43 contradicted requirement 128 then they were bound to deliver it with this flawed logic. When you have a contract, you have to deliver what is in the contract or you risk not being paid if either requirement 43 or 128 are not delivered. Perversely there is even an incentive not to correct it because when you handed over to the customer and they find the flaw, they are going to have to pay you extra money to correct it. I saw a wonderful example of this in one organisation I worked with. They had put out for competitive tendering the development of an application. An Israeli company won the bid, meetings ensued, contracts were signed, and everything looked rosy until nine months later when the software was delivered for user acceptance testing. The slight problem the user acceptance testers had was that all the screens were in Hebrew with the labels naturally for Hebrew on the right-hand side. When the distressed managers raised this with the supplier, they were able to point out that nowhere in the contract did it state that the screens were to be in English.

Legally correct they were able to extract more money from the organisation to redo all the screens into English.

This highlights three problems that arise from this method of software delivery. Firstly restricting ourselves to the letter of the contract can allow bugs in workflows and unusable software to be developed and signed off as technically correct to the wording of the contract. We also see a disincentive for the supplier to point out any errors or bugs in the system. By only showing the software to the customer near the very end of the process we inhibit the ability for the customer to have any input or correct any errors, in fact even if we do spot something early, we will be restricted by the contract from making changes. Finally, if the customer wants working software, they end up having to fork out the extra cash and generally, this reworking also delays delivery. By deliberately delaying showing the customer any progress we increase the chance, as a supplier, of the customer having to pay us more money through change controls. This is where a cobra analogy comes in, a process that is intended to keep to the budget and deliver on time is riddled with incentives for the supplier to wait to the last minute to show you anything so that they can increase the possibility of getting changes approved which will result in more revenue and for yourself longer waiting times for delivery.

Now let us not kid ourselves that delivering projects internally solves all these problems. At another organisation, there was a question raised about whether as the costs increased there was a business case to be made for continuing with particular software development. The project manager, not me in this case, was asked to present a paper for consideration. This is the turkeys voting for Christmas scenario. If you ask a project manager whether the project, they are on should be cancelled with the resulting loss of status and questions around potential job security, what do you think their answer is going to be. There are the same incentives for internal teams to do the same thing, just without the lawyers and the contracts. They can equally say we built it to the requirements, ask for change controls and get extra money allocated to the budget. I have never seen an internal project team go to the pub in mourning after work to decry the fact that their team has been asked to stay together and continue delivery for another three or six months. Change brings uncertainty and even if we're not ecstatically happy with what we are doing it is less stressful for our brains to continue doing what we are doing rather than face uncertainty, which would be the case if the project ends.

Please note that none of the above discussions is in any way focused on delivering good quality software. The whole purpose of MSP and Prince2 is to deliver on time and on budget. Any high school child studying algebra will tell you in a three-factor equation if two of the items are fixed and only the third can be a variable then only the variable can be changed, which in our case means quality. It is strange is it not, that when we are presented with waterfall projects no one mentions that to fix the budget and timescales we will reduce the quality of the product. I wonder why that is not highlighted more often?

Alternatively in Agile you will work with the team to define all the new features that you want, and we will prioritise those as; must-haves, should haves, could haves and finally won't have. There are other methods of scoring this but generally, the principle is that we prioritise what needs to be delivered. This is our starting point, and we fully accept that as we show the progress that people will ask for tweaks and changes, and it is almost certain that somewhere through the delivery someone is going to suddenly remember some process or connection to data that was missed in the original planning. Note to the mind of some ardent waterfall project managers this may sound like chaos on the other hand it could be considered that you are dealing with reality rather than fantasy. It could be argued that to assume at the beginning we have absolute perfect knowledge, no one will ever look at the products and suggest a change or there will be any external or internal factors that may impact your delivery could be considered a fantasy.

If you do not have a product team, then you should effectively invent them. It is the usual process of beg borrow and stealing the skills you need, cobbling together a disparate set of people with different ways of working and hoping they can pull together as a team. This is where things are going to change. When we work in Agile the team will analyse, develop and test within a small, fixed window of two to four weeks. In the end, we are going to demonstrate what we have produced to the customer and hopefully get their sign off. We can also expect that there may be some changes requested like "is it possible to also capture the age" or more aesthetic things like "could we have a lighter shade of blue". These new items are going to be prioritised and added to a backlog. They will get picked up by the team based on the priority of the request. This is where the product owner comes in. From all the things which the customers asked for which of them is most important for them to see next. I have over the years been surprised about what the customer thinks is a priority. Some organisations focused on marketing and brand identity, things like the shade of blue are highly important for them whereas, I who am more data and logically inclined would have thought that the data capture of the age would be a more important priority. Between the product owner the team and the customer, we agree on what is technically possible to do and what is our priority for the next sprint. This process will repeat and repeat and repeat until we have delivered everything the customer wants to the point that the items which are in the backlog do not justify the cost of keeping the team working on it or the money runs out.

It is important to grasp the concept that some things may not be delivered. This is not necessarily because we're wanting to be cruel and nasty. Some of the things which the customer asks us for do not give us bang for buck or the organisation any real value.

An example of this is a situation where I had an Agile team make a change to a workflow for an educational client. Being an educational client, they had surges in applications that are associated with the academic year. We had automated one workflow and the customer was highly delighted that a lot of manual processing had been removed and everything was working well. This led them to ask whether we could do the same for another area, which we looked at and tried to assess the value. What I asked the customer was what do you do currently. They replied that they hired two or three temporary data entry staff for two weeks to manually capture the data. When I did my calculations, I worked out how much it was going to cost to deliver then divided it by the cost of hiring the temporary workers. The figures showed that the software would need to be in operation for 32.2 years for it to break even. My advice which was accepted was that it was too expensive to automate this workflow and it would not return any real value to the business.

Not everything that is asked for is a must-have. One of the problems we have had generated out of decades of waterfall software delivery is that our customers are getting wise to it. They know that while there is a budget available and a project team it is their turn on the swings. They had better get as much as they can out of this because it can be any time between two to ten years before anybody looks at the software again. There is a point that I will bring up when you look at analysis teams, we ask the wrong questions. If I bring back my nine-year-old son again and ask what you want for Christmas I will get a list that would fill two pages. When we asked people what they want, we get one answer when we asked people, what do you need? we get a different answer. If we are going to deliver based on value, then we need to determine the must-haves compared to the could or should have.

I have a very simple measure for a must-have, it is a bit brutal however it is fairly effective. I ask the following question, "if this feature or item is not available at 9 AM on the day that we go live will we pull the deployment and cancel the release of the software". If you get any answer other than an absolute affirmative yes it must be there, then it is not a must-have the slightest hesitation or well maybe... will indicate to you that is not a true must-have. A more academic description of a must-have would be that the user of the system cannot complete the user journey that is intended to be deployed with this release, or some backend processing cannot be completed. Maybe other considerations you want to add could be security, marketing or such like things, but the basics are that when you present a bit of software to the user, they should be able to use it and that the data that is captured should be usable. We will continue to deliver and deploy additional functionality each sprint until the point where there is no value to deliver anymore.

I have had it countered that everything we have is a must-have and therefore Agile will not work. Even in highly regulated markets like banks the "requirements" while mandatory always have several ways to satisfy them. Let's look at an example that may sound very rigid.

"A customer must have the ability to recall a direct debit payment from their account within 90 days of the payment being taken from their account"

Ok, this sounds very specific and a must-have but how we do it may be done in a myriad of ways.

1. Go to your branch and ask for it to be done over the counter
2. Download a form from our website, print it and post it back to us
3. Have a web form that the customer can fill in.
4. Add it as a menu item to the customers online banking to request a recall.

5. Have a recall item available on the mobile app
6. Allow the customer the option to use telephone banking to make the request
7. Tell the customer they must send in a written, dated and signed request by post

You may choose one or all of these to satisfy your must-have "requirement". So even in the most regulated markets we have options on how we do it, each will have value to the customer and us and we need to make a judgement call based on the priorities of this "requirement"

As a sideline, I do not like the term REQUIREMENT. You require to breathe oxygen every 4 minutes, or you will have brain death, you require food every seven days, or you will start to have organ failure. I have seen too many so-called requirements that have landed in the trash can when money and time were tight. Therefore, they were not requirements were they. Try and avoid the word, it has a meaning in the English language which is not appropriate when discussing software development.

While this process is going on sprint after sprint the project manager is going to have to do is to throw out a lot of existing paperwork that we have. It is not always that it does not exist but rather it is replaced with something new. Imagine if you will, you replace your petrol car with an electric car. I will not go to the gas station to top up I will plug it into the electricity grid. I do not have a conventional exhaust pipe because the electric engine does not have any exhausts therefore the assumption that I will have to replace some or all my exhaust within 50,000 miles is no longer true.

When can we start the project?

Another big question is when we can start. I normally answer yesterday. There is a fundamental approach different to that used by waterfall. If I accept the following as true, and I cannot see why not then this lets us start right away.

I will never have perfect knowledge of what the current system does.

The customer will change their mind.

The change will appear from things outside the project because the rest of the world is not static while we are doing our bit.

The customer will normally ask for more than time or money will allow.

If some or most of that rings true with yourself then it kind of highlights what a futile and complete waste of money all this upfront month of analysis is. It is supposed to define a fixed deliverable with a fixed cost and timescale. Reality tells you that you are doomed from the start. We do like our fantasies, however, because they give us comfort and false reassurance that we do not need to deal with the nasty realities of the world. If you are one of the processes focused, I nearly became an accountant type of project manager all this dealing with reality is going to be problematic. It usually comes with talk about correct process and procedure, but I can read between the lines and what you are telling me is "I have built a career out of building fantasies, and then getting paid to do paperwork when they don't work and create new fantasy's just a bit more expensive and longer than the last one. I then wander off into the sunset until the next healthy dose of reality hits, when I can do it all over again". At this point, I like to explore it a bit more by using the analogy of a wedding.

When your beloved goes down on one knee and says, "will you make me the happiest person in the world and do me the honour of marrying me?", you do not expect the answer to be "how can I possibly answer that without knowing whether auntie Jean will sit next to uncle George at the wedding reception". When we do major things in our lives like moving house, getting a new job or marrying we accept that when we start into the process, we are not going to know everything, and we will need to learn and modify the plans as we go. Magically as soon as we cross the entrance of the office that form of reality disappears and is replaced with a different quantum state in which every particle within the office is stationary, its spin and direction are known and the quantum physicist can predict everything, I don't think so.

When a couple agreed to get married after the initial excitement and possibly a kiss or two, the planning can begin. We have a final goal in mind, how we get it is a bit vague at the moment. Couples will discuss with themselves some fairly basic questions. Do we want a big wedding or a small wedding, should it be a registry office or at church? Depending on the answers to these, it will give us a guide on whether you are going to have a reception.

The reception has multiple questions. What is to be on the menu, are we going to have live music and so on down to what colour of linen and flowers should we have on the tables. If you're going to have a reception, then you need to decide where people will sit. If auntie Jean and Uncle George had divorced, should they be sitting next to each other or is it better to be diplomatic and put them at different tables? By the time we get to look at the options for any vegan or vegetarian menu, you are getting close to having most things settled.

We do not see in real life that we put off the decision to marry-until the seating plans and the colour of the bridesmaid's dresses, the selection of the hymns is decided. We do things step-by-step and sometimes will have to make compromises when one venue for the reception may have wonderful views and a great menu but is smaller and you need to compromise on the number of guests. If any of the readers have been married, they will not be surprised that it can take up to a year to plan everything and get to the final wedding day. What we do not do is sit down and document everything for six months, get it ratified before agreeing to get married. We just need to know enough to move on to the next step. "Yes, I will marry you, I always wanted a church wedding and I would like to have a reception with all my family and friends there". I have enough to start looking at venues speaking to clergymen and thinking of a possible guestlist. The decisions I make here will then form part of my decision-making for the next steps. I find this quite a useful analogy as to how Agile works. If you're working on a two-week cycle, then at the bare minimum all you need to know is what you do for the next two weeks and then you can start.

Agile also appreciates that written communications are not always the best way to express your desires and while I accept that many great writers have had a good stab at it. If written communications were the best way to pass on requirements, then let me ask you this. If you have ever been to university or college, did they say to you here is your reading list, the library is over there, come back in four years and sit an exam. Most students find that this is not the case, and the teaching is supplemented with lectures, workshops and tutorials. This is because universities and colleges recognise dealing with just purely written material and not supplementing it can lead to misunderstandings and misinterpretations. The written requirements are the last resort if you have no other way to communicate with your customer. Virtually all Agile projects replace requirement documentation with small compact stories. So, this is yet another piece of documentation that you do not need to create or maintain.

There is often a visual aspect to software and here the saying a picture tells a thousand words is true. You will not believe the number of times when I have gone with a sketched-out mock-up of what is clearly defined specifically in a written document even down to positional sizes at points of a millimetre. When I show the client, I get the feedback "can this be moved here, can this go to the bottom of the page. I think it would be better if this was split over two pages" and so on. It is not too surprising even with a simple wireframe we are connecting to different parts of the client's brain, and they are then making different connections in their brain that they did not do with the written word. These new connections bring out new questions and ideas, which they request to be added to the signed off, final and definitive version. That should be the final and definitive version that you have just shredded and ask for all those changes to be applied. I do not worry about these things, it is intentional. I want to get all this found out at the start, so I do not waste time building it all and then getting the feedback and have all that nonsense with the paperwork associated with change controls. By doing this a couple of times over a few weeks I have often found I have a much better idea of what the client wants without three to six months of requirements gathering. The observant amongst you will have noted the scant reference to change controls. There is no need for them. The client should know the financial parameters. We have six months of funding for this team. If you want to spend that time writing the front screen in two hundred shades of pink so you can pick the one that best suits your complexion then it is your money you are spending. You will end up with a fabulous front screen with the most wonderful shade of pink but nothing else. As the client determines the priority in the backlog, with the guidance of the team and the product owner then every sprint planning session is a form of change management. You have to decide what is the next most important feature to add or amend in your system. It is agreed and signed off as the deliverables for the next sprint. The chain of command does not go up to the project board it stays with the customer. Remember that person we are supposed to be delivering this for.

Here is a really big point. If we start with let's write down the big things you want this to do. Like the wedding. Then say which is the most important. For this item, we can break it down even with post-it notes on the wall into smaller bits of functionality like login, view items for sale, add to basket and finally check out. This is enough for us to get started. A day or two later we present a wireframe of what that log on screen should look like. The feedback may need some changes and we are back again in a further two days with the revised layout. Great we have agreement. Now we will break that down into little functional parts like entering a username, entering a password, what error messages should we see, should we have a forgotten password option and so on. Sign these little bits off and we are ready to start coding in two weeks. While the coders and testers are busy with the login screen, we start again with the view items. Here we have started coding what will be part of the final product within two to three weeks. Waterfall just cannot compete. It will never catch up with the time difference of three to six months and I have even seen eighteen months for the analysis stage and sign off. Agile can at the extreme end be done and live before waterfall has got the low-level requirements signed off. The lack of bureaucracy and direct contact with the customer reduces misunderstanding and that classic 30% of dev and test time that is spent on rework is reduced to something like 5 or 10%. With the final flourish that when we are at the end we are done, not at the UAT stage when we will wait to bug fix. I am going to save 20% of the project time at the end and

20% of the effort from rework. Add to this that I am starting production coding ages earlier there is just no way waterfall can compete on time, price or quality. If you are a day rate project manager as I have been then this is a bit of bad news. You will not be able to milk that budget for eighteen months in seven or eight it is going to be delivered and you will be looking for your next project. On the other hand, it is pretty good news for the customer and the business so at least someone is happy.

The project plan is replaced with a prioritised backlog, so no project plan. Equally our checkpoint reports either weekly or monthly also go. The purpose of these is supposed to be to report to the business on our progress. This becomes completely pointless when the team demonstrates real-time progress to the business every two weeks. The business can see for themselves with their own eyes. The team will monitor progress every working day at the stand-up. If somebody is interested enough to want to know the details of what's going on in your project, then invite them to the stand-up. Especially if the team is using some form of electronic sprint board, the information is available in real-time all the time. If you want to know where a particular feature is, have a look at the board the information is there for you. Most organisations below the executive level have done away with the secretarial class. It was once thought that a manager was not capable of filling in their calendar or taking notes at a meeting without somebody to do the admin for them. We have replaced such functions with applications like Microsoft Outlook. The days of reporting historical data which in most cases is out of date in what is effectively a replica of a paper format should be in the past. As I indicated the team are going to remain as a team and work through the deliveries in a just-in-time format. One of the interesting things this does for financial reporting is to effectively remove the need for financial reporting. If I have an Agile team of seven and they are dedicated to it full time then my costs are fixed last week, this week and the next. What is there to report on.

One of the interesting things from this model of working that scares several people is the absolute openness of the process. It is quite possible in the waterfall method to have any number of difficulties, screw-ups and failures and to keep them effectively hidden. If we do not need to show our workings for a further six months, we can blindly continue in the hope that somehow between then and now it will all magically come together. In Agile the assumption is everybody knows everything. This is not that Agile has more problems and it certainly does not. But when the team come across something which is blocking them from progress, they highlight it and do everything within the power of the team to fix it or escalate it as required. The basic difference here is that with Agile you know about the problems. These problems were going to exist like compatibility of software components or a lack of capacity in infrastructure it is just under waterfall they would have been hidden from your view until it became a crisis. With Agile we hope to identify these things as early as possible as part of de-risking the project to give as much time to find a solution. This means they find out about the same problems but just earlier.

The way we measure progress needs to change as well. Because a lot of the waterfall deliveries of very financially budget-focused, they very often fall into a trend of reporting financial results as actual results. We are 50% of the way through a twelve-month project therefore we must have spent 50% of the budget, which is not an unreasonable assertion to be made by the finance department and this can be tested against real figures if you wished. The problem comes when we associate that bums on seats equals deliveries. I worked on some projects where we have spent 20% of the time and delivered 60% of the functionality. Conversely, I worked on other projects where 80% of the time has been used and only 40% of the functionality is available. We need to stop what is quite an irrational assumption that having burnt through 50% of the allocated resource budget this some way equates to 50% of the delivery.

Most Agile teams adopt a form of comparative estimation. If you think of your house and you are trying to plan redecoration then we may be able to use the differences in the size of rooms to give ourselves some indication of how much time it is going to take us to redecorate. If the guest bedroom is half the size of the master bedroom, then we may be able to estimate that the master bedroom is going to take us twice as long. Within Agile we like to base our comparisons on things that we have already delivered and have good knowledge about. Therefore, as a team continues and progresses, they will get better and better at comparing the size of one job against another. This method of estimating generally comes in as an order of magnitude four times better than the quantitative estimating that is normally done. It is also reviewed by the team throughout the delivery as part of the continuous improvement to try and get better and better. It is quite typical for us to give this a numerical value, one of the most common being the Fibonacci sequence. As a project manager, you can probably take a hands-off approach to this, but you do want to know what the outcome is. The team will measure the actual progress of delivery and using story points as a form of measure we will be able to give accurate results. The maths is simple if the team can deliver 30 points of work in a sprint and we have 300 points in a backlog then we are going to need ten sprints to complete. It is as simple as that. No smoke and mirrors, no estimates or guesstimates, timelines based on empirical fact. The only way that this is going to change is if the team can increase its delivery rate which may or may not be possible or reduce the size of the backlog. When we are halfway through a project we can look and see if indeed we have delivered 150 points, either we have or we have not. They have not then we can ask why and there may be a good reason technically, but it leads us to ask the question why. The team's delivery cannot and will not be the same each sprint as they are not robots, this is why we take rolling averages. I was once charged with an Agile team to give a delivery date which I did use this method I estimated that we would complete by about 2:30 in the afternoon on the 14th of the following month.

I was unfortunately found to be incorrect in my estimation it turned out that we finished up at 12:30 in the afternoon two hours earlier.

We need to accept that the backlog may shrink or grow during the lifetime of the project. This is not always a negative thing. I have seen cases where during a demonstration of a particular screen or webpage the customer has liked what we have done so much that they have asked if that same feature or element can be replicated in other parts of the application. The answer is always in theory, yes and it can be added to the backlog. However, when it gets done depends on a) it is technically possible to do at the time, b) you as a customer prioritise this item is having enough value to be picked up by the team before everything else in the backlog. This has implications for the business as they will be asked what is the next thing you want us to pick up. If they prioritise the shading of blue on the screen over-reporting or automating email to customers, then that is their choice. If you're working with a fixed budget, make your customer abundantly aware that they can prioritise whatever they want but in the end, they will need to accept that what is delivered is what they prioritised. This way of working is fairly straightforward and has quite a lot of common sense in it, but to your average waterfall project manager, it can be a big psychological jump. An analogy I use is that of a catering company used to planning weddings with a fixed menu and a possible vegetarian option, life becomes relatively simple when it is only the quantity of guests which can change. If on the other hand, the catering company is a restaurant then we do not know whether the customer is going to order fish or pasta or for that matter how many customers, we will have this evening. There are a lot of successful restaurants and multinational food chains like McDonald's out there living in a world where customers can make choices is not a business model which is completely alien. It just needs a different mindset.

To summarise for the project manager ideally, you're going to have a product team in place if not you are going to create one. The team is not going to frontload the analysis or backend the testing, everything is going to be done in real-time. This makes life easier because you have a fixed cost of resources throughout the lifetime of the project which in turn makes financial reporting really easy or even pointless to do. A lot of planning and traditional reporting is pointless when you have a backlog and monitor progress using Agile boards either physical or electronic. We have quantifiable real data points in story points to give factual information about progress. The customer is going to sign off the priorities for the next sprint and because of that, you have to accept that when a particular feature is available, depending on the customer or their representative the product owner. Interestingly one of the things which infuriate most project managers about Agile is when they ask will XYZ be available on the 16th of next month to which the scrum master will answer if the product owner and the customer agree that XYZ is important enough to be in the next sprint then it will be ready, however, if they do not feel it is important enough to be included in the next sprint it will not be. Therefore, if you wish this feature to be available on the 16th of next month then you had better speak to the product owner and the customer and emphasise to them why it is a priority and valuable for them to have it included in the next sprint. This is a subtle and devious change for the project manager. Many of us will including myself have been used to telling people that they must have X and it will need to be done by Y. The concept that the customer that we are delivering this product to is in charge of the process is quite a deep and fundamental one for us to get our heads around. It is however no more unusual than to assume that the prioritisation for software delivery should somehow be organised and arranged by the finance department. We can't go around claiming we are customer-focused organisations if we don't want to listen to our customers.

Many of the hardened project managers of the waterfall variety will be thinking to themselves "aha you have missed out on risks and issues" certainly that's true for risks however I have indicated about issues. The team at the daily stand-up will highlight any issues sometimes called blockers, which are preventing them from making progress because they are working to a very short timescale sometimes just two weeks. They will move heaven and earth and want to get things done quickly so that they can deliver everything for their sprint. The typical waterfall process as a project manager is to log an issue in our issue log whether that is paper-based or electronic. We then report said issues in weekly or monthly reports to the finance department and the project offices and sometimes to the customer or project board. If the issue or risk is realised and impacts delivery, we will ask the team to stop what they're doing and do an analysis of what the impact is, what the options are and prophetically also include timescales and costs for implementing these options. We can then formulate a change control with a recommendation for the appropriate option to choose and the costs are submitted for financial and business approval. When the said control has been approved, we then go to the finance department and ensure that they have allocated the appropriate sum of money associated with the change control to our project budget. When the additional finances are secured, we then attempt to schedule the change. The observant amongst you will have noticed one small element of truth in all of that process. None of that actually did anything to resolve the issue. In fact, by asking the team to focus on estimating the impact rather than trying to fix it we have probably impeded progress even further. In Agile we want issues identified upfront and dealt with right away. If the team cannot do it then you need to escalate it and that's where you come in as the project manager, if another team is telling them it is going to be six weeks to get some component that our team needs then it's your job to go and apply whatever hard or soft pressure you can on the other team to move forward the delivery. Therefore, our issue log is our current list of blockers, it does not become any less blocked because I have also recorded it in a spreadsheet. Issues are in real-time recorded as blockers and can change daily; in this way, our blocked items list is our issue log.

Next comes the question of risks, risk management in itself can be useful and there is no harm in looking at the potential risks that delivery faces and whether we have any options or mitigations should those risks be realised. NASA take this to extremes where they will game out what could happen with a spacecraft halfway to the moon. The question for the Agile team is where the responsibility for monitoring these risks lies. Traditionally the workstream teams maintain their risk logs and the project manager will cherry-pick which ones to be included in the project reporting. There is a new adage that I would like to introduce into the business world. Developers are best at coding; analysts are best at analysing and testers are best at testing. This indicates that anything we asked the team to do which is not based around the key skills for delivery is sub-optimal. There is very little point in asking a team to maintain a risk log particularly if the risks pertain to things that they have no control over such as restrictions on infrastructure availability or timelines for delivery by other teams or suppliers. It is fine for the team to raise the risk but the management monitoring and reporting of the risk should be with the project manager or their equivalent within the project office. Critically it is interactions with other teams and access to their resource pools that cause the most risk and issues. This is where your new role is to become a resource manager with the other teams. Ensure that you have the appropriate funding if required and mechanisms for your team to call off time with the other teams. Earn your wages by preventing blockers rather than reporting on them.

Projects with Product Teams

If you're lucky your organisation will already have put in place product teams. These will be groups of individuals who have the necessary skills to support and maintain the application or a portfolio of small applications. They are the best people to implement any changes your project wants to implement. The problem we have is a very simple one, they are usually only funded and resourced for the bare minimum support and maintenance tasks. More IT-savvy organisations are realising that with a modest increase in the size of these teams and keeping them together they then can also take on project work. The pros here for the project manager is that we can jump right past the analysis stage largely and start the conversation at the point where we describe the changes we would like to implement. This team knows the product and are not going to need large chunks of time to analyse and document the existing system. This is our first big saving in the process.

The best way to organise these product teams this to keep them together. You know that some sports and many human activities that teams, once formed perform better when they get to know each other, and they increase understanding of how each other works. One of the biggest failures of teams is they don't have the resources to deliver the things themselves and there beholding on others so as much as practically possible ensure that the team has the right mix of skills to deliver what you're asking them to do. Where you need specialists like security people or infrastructure teams allocate them to the team. It can make common sense and you don't have to be long-winded about it. Get a group of people together and make them responsible for something as they go through the code, test and fix, all the way to deployment and support beyond. If your team is quiet for a while, please never pull individuals out to do other work, that destroys the team.

Alternatively, give new work for the team to do. We kick off a project and we go around the organisation like a pack of hungry wolves working each of the flocks of sheep seeing which ones we can devour. When you pull people away from what they are normally doing it is very disruptive. There is a learning curve which will normally be two to six weeks of inefficiency while they get up to speed. When you bring a new person to the organisation, they normally take three to six months to get up to speed. Ironically adding people to a team in the short term often reduces productivity as the experienced team members have to dedicate time to the newbies to train them. Meanwhile, the team or department for which they have been plucked sadly has a whole and they are having to backfill and have all the same problems. There is a high-efficiency cost of moving people around so once your team is formed keep it together.

Decide which service or services I am going to include in the scope of the product team. For some things, this will be simple. If you run a chain of hotels, then the room booking system may be seen as a service which we offer the customers and can be supported by a product team. Any project-related changes can be handed to this team to deliver, financial chargebacks for the time or percentage of their work for the delivery of this project can be accommodated, thus enabling us to take advantage of the tax breaks given in some jurisdictions for capital investment in software.

How is this going to look and feel different from what we do now? A lot of organisations talk about cross-functional teams, unfortunately for the people working in the said cross-functional teams, it can feel like everybody is my boss. If I use my example of the hotel room booking system where I get my product team together. I may need three developers and three testers an analyst, DBA and possibly a part-time scrum master, product owner and networks person. These people are going to be assigned to the product probably a minimum of three years. Welcome and get used to your sole purpose in life is to make sure that this product works and is updated. If anything comes along that is project related, then you deliver and recharge through your timesheets. In a simple slash of the pen, we have removed all the traditional project kick-off processes because we don't need to analyse the current functionalities. The product team supporting the product already have all this information.

Having things put into neat little buckets makes it easier for finance, these buckets are called budget codes. With projects, we spend 10 to 25% of the cost of project monitoring to make sure things are kept in their bucket. Then we rip resources away to resource the project and be assigned to the budget code. We are asked to report deliveries based on financial quarters or year ends. Quite frankly my customers that book hotel rooms don't give a flying monkey behind that it is the end of our second-quarter reporting period. We create projects and backfill them with resources, delivering to team skills that are not customer focused to suit the pleasure of the finance department. I'm not trying to get at the finance department here but if I was going to ask which department would be best to understand and organise the delivery of software to our customers you probably would not pick the finance department. It is surprising that in so many organisations there is a finance department that controls how we deliver software. I have observed often the structure we place around project delivery has a direct correlation to the finance hierarchy in place.

The finance department needs to allocate the costs to whichever bucket it likes, that is its job after all. We should not be trying to form our teams to match particular budgets. In the retail world, we know that each shop needs a certain number of staff to keep the premises open. We may want to supplement these with weekend workers or extra staff at busy periods like Christmas but in general, we have a core team with all the skills to run the shop and they are responsible for that outlet. We know that this financial model works, so it is not too hard for us to think about applying this financial model to the support of a product rather than a shop

Do not be afraid to challenge the product owner or the customer if you think something is not a must-have and get close to your scrum master and find out what the blockers are that the team are facing and remove them. If you are working in a program and need your team to deliver something that someone else is using, then it is your job to convince the product owner and the customer that it is important enough to prioritise. They are rightly focused on their delivery and do not be surprised if they do not care too much that the mobile team have a twelve-week lead time. They may ask why "they don't adopt Agile and stop handing their problems to other people". It has often surprised me why some other team's inability to adequately resource their team for the predicted workload should be my problem. If anyone gives you a lead time of more than 2 weeks or one sprint if it is bigger, then they have a problem in their department and that needs to be sorted out.

Testing, Analysis and Development

When talking about Agile I commonly like to use the testing department because it is relatively easy for most people to understand what they do, which is test. Also, it exemplifies a number of the changes which will be asked for by Agile. Team managers in some departments like testing are used to being asked for resources but it is a different matter when we say I want two testers for the next three to five years. At this point the traditional line manager relationship becomes pointless. I have seen testing line managers doing annual staff reviews with people they physically have not seen for nine months because they have been assigned to a product team. We mentioned earlier in the book that there are clear benefits in building teams to deliver products. As the head of a testing department, your life is spent juggling demand for testers, that demand often changes and as we are at the end of the line any delays accumulate into what available time we have. Typically, the project will come to you saying "we're running two weeks late but can you still do all the testing". The answer should be no, there is no reason to assume that because you are running late that somebody else can miraculously deliver all the functionality within less time. I was once asked on a traditional waterfall project by a business I was working with for various operational reasons they did not think they could give us the requirements for a bit of software delivery on time. When I inquired how long it was going to be they estimated it was going to take them an additional six months. My stock reply was that they would then get the software six months later unless the expected requirements were going to be substantially less than what was in the current scope. There was much chagrin to this reply as it was thought unreasonable in some quarters where a six-month delay in starting a project should result in a six-month delay in delivering it. I stood by my timescales in the end I was proven correct. So much of your life as the testing manager is spent dealing with resource requirements that change or if the project is running late, they ask if we can throw more people at it, to which the answer is of course I keep some spare testers in this cupboard ready to pull out for any such emergencies. It will take me an hour or two to give them a cup of coffee and for their eyes to adjust to the light but by the end of the day, they should be fully functional. If only it was that easy.

Now let's look at the Agile product team. We estimate that this product needs two testers to support it. The product team is going to be in place for three years. I have some specific technical skills needed. The resource management holiday management and delivery management are all handed over to the Agile team. Also, we want the testers to be collocated with the rest of the team because that gives the best results. The team has to deal with the demand fluctuation, the team is also responsible for allocating work around holidays, the team is responsible for ensuring the quality of the testing along with the customers who sign off this and the team is responsible for the delivery schedules, not the department head.

As this carries on other department heads start to notice that more and more seats are empty as the testers go off and join the new teams. It is not long before other department heads start to look enviously at all that lovely space you have and start asking questions about whether they could borrow a seat or two from you. Your contact with your testers is reduced sometimes to as little as agreement on departmental standards, which becomes a bit of a joke when you don't have anybody in your department and doing annual appraisals for which you have no direct evidence about what they have been doing. Occasionally you will get an email requesting you to approve a holiday, as you don't know what their workload is you will probably approve assuming that they have talked it through with the team.

Some managers assume their worth equates to the number of people working for them directly. If my department has one hundred and twenty people, then I must be more important than your department that has fifty. As your testing staff disappear to the teams it becomes less obvious what size department you manage. You run the risk of appearing less important. There are a few ways you can deal with this. Go with the flow and look on the bright side, life is so much simpler without all that resource scheduling. While this might work in the short term it is liable to be noticed eventually that is the fear that somebody may ask why we are paying for this department head if there does not appear to be anybody in the department. Which is a reasonable question somebody is going to ask eventually. If you are worried about your perceived loss of importance you can always try and block it, play hardball and slow down the inevitable. If we block our staff from moving to the projects our product teams will recruit contractors directly and the cost overruns are going to be blamed on you and why you were not able to deliver the resources in the first place. If you hold on to your permanent staff, then the Agile teams were hired in contract freelancers and the question this time will be if the contractors are doing all the work and all the permanent staff are sitting around twiddling their collective thumbs what the point of the whole department and not just a department head.

This is a real threat to yourself and the comfortable way of life you and your partner have come to enjoy recently. You could use this as an opportunity to restructure your department. There are all those quality standards that you wanted to introduce and be adopted or there may be the automation of testing that you never had time to deal with. Can you justify your job by being the person who improves the quality and implements innovative technologies to speed up the process? In this way, your job role changes from managing resources to managing quality and ensuring that your team department has the best and right tools available to them. This is not going to be a comfortable journey, but it is a useful one to be deployed in the organisation and justifiable. Those who can adapt will no longer be measured by the number of bums on seats but rather by the number of automated tests available, simplification of processes. Can we justify our existence as the person who improves quality? If not start polishing up your resume and hope that you can get a few good years in at the next place before Agile arrives there.

The head of development is going to face the same ask. We want people to join our teams that they will live eat and breathe as part of that team. When the people are gone you need to manage the technology choices, when should we upgrade to that new version of the code repository. You will end up managing the tooling the teams use. Your focus is on best quality and performance or being able to hook in automated tests, what is our process if an automated test or build fails. You will migrate to managing the glue that keeps the developers working rather than managing people. Same story in the Analyst world but even more so. No more requirements documents or the requirements gathering, with all those associated templates. Rather what is the best tool for us to create wireframes? How do we improve the quality of our stories? Testers still test and developers code just in a different way, For the analysis team this is a complete job rewrite and fundamental change to what and how we determine what the customer wants.

As I am old enough, I remember when computers started to arrive in offices, first the typing pools disappeared when word processing and multicopy printing arrived on the scene. There used to be professional clerical and secretarial workers which were replaced in most instances with email and calendars which were self-service. If you are not going to go the same way you will need to look at where you can add value to the business and sell yourself as the one to deliver it. Often this is all the items you had on your to-do list but never reasonably had time to do when you had all those people to manage. Well, the people are gone so you have time to polish off all those items on your wish list and start implementing them. You have a real advantage here; you are already on the books and paid for. This means that you just need to justify your value. Start polishing off all those ideas that were going to improve things, make the process easier and all-around add value and quality to the organisation. If you accept the challenge and embrace it, you have a good chance of keeping your job.

Project with Project Teams

The basic mechanics of how you run the team and the artefacts that they produce will be the same as for a product team. The difference being you will need to hand the team back at the point where the project is delivered. They will go through an adjustment phase back to their old job or on to another project team with the usual drop in productivity associated with a move. The business will just take the hit as always and lose 10-50% productivity during the transition. That is not your concern you have a project to deliver and if the organisation that is hiring you wants to work in a sub-optimal manner that is not your concern. I have stated in the past if the client wants me to go to the roof and throw laptops into the car park, as long as we have covered the health and safety side, I will do it. I will advise against it but ultimately the client is the boss.

You want all the team there, for all of the project, yes, we have our tendencies as project managers to shave a few days off here and there in the resource pool but do not do it. Think of a retail model. When we have a Starbucks or Apple shop, they have a staffing level that is needed to be there all the time. That is a retail model. Yes, you can ask if everyone needs to be in at 9 am but the basics are that a shop needs people. That is treated financially as a fixed cost for the retail outlet. I need a barista, one person serving and another on the till. They all hand off to each other and you cannot take one away without affecting the delivery.

You will have difficult discussions with line managers as you look to effectively remove people from the line managers team and move them physically to your team. Post covid it may sound odd but there needs to be a psychological break from I am one of twenty testers assigned work to I am a member of this team, and my focus is on delivering for the customer and the team. If you leave them back at their old desk, they will be dragged back to help out anytime there is a problem back in the old department. I would rather have someone working from home, at least that is a psychological break rather than remain at their old desk.

Your prime role is no longer an organiser as that is done between the team and the customer. You should focus on removing potential blockers. This usually but not always is about resources and processes. If there has not been a trailblazer before you need to start knocking heads together to get the appropriate monitoring and reporting in place with finance and the PMO. I remember starting at a new client and I asked where the stationery cupboard was because I wanted a few post-it notes and marker pens for a whiteboard. I was directed to the said cupboard and the guardian of the treasure trove informed me that I needed to note down what had been taken and which budget code it was to be allocated to. Only having been on the client's site an hour or so I did not know the budget code. Several phone calls later and a trip with three people in tow we arrived at the PMO who were able to supply the code. I am sure this process is intended to prevent waste. Whenever we have an audit trail it is either for security or to track costs. However, I wondered to myself if the generous day rate I was on at the time and given the time I had spent in this process it may have been possible to have purchased the contents of the cupboard with what I had just charged the client for my efforts to get post-it notes.

When we ask how you do X, you often get to fill in form B and then get it signed off by your line manager. If you ask what you are trying to achieve and we get an answer like monitor project deliveries, then that opens up the conversation on how story points are not only perfectly adequate for the task but more accurate. Please do not be afraid to challenge what the finance and PMO traditionally want. Your job now is to remove blockers and if unnecessary or inappropriate paperwork is one of these blockers then that is your job to remove it. You also need to resource specialists like security, networks and any other number of people that will tie it all together. Identify them as a named person and get them to your stand-ups. I like to use a fixed amount of time per week, Say 1 day per week. This is understandable at a human level and the person knows they have to commit that time. There will be variation but when you have this type of commitment you will get steady progress, not fits and starts and black holes when nobody is available. You are delivering regularly so there should be an expectation from supporting teams that they will also be required regularly.

The customer knows what they want, the team know what is possible and finances tell us how many weeks we have to burn. Stand aside and let the customer and the team deliver. Get all the nonsense, paperwork and blockers out of the way. This is a psychological adjustment that some project managers cannot make, they are just too used to ordering people about and demanding that the widget must be delivered by the first of the month. If you cannot make the mental step from Captain to a servant, then unfortunately it is time to start looking at the job market. Some organisations still retain the Project managers and PMO and layer on the Agile, but realistically if your role is diminished to a servant to smooth the way for delivery then you will be able to handle more than one project. Do the maths most Project Managers in the Agile world juggle two to four projects because of the light touch needed. When it is no longer a one to one relationship, we will need fewer project managers. There is only so long you can sit staring at a spreadsheet doing nothing before someone notices. You can either adapt and accept the new project manager role or move on. It is normally a rate of one PM kept and two let go after one year. You may want to be the one who remains.

Would you like bugs with that

When Agile kicks in people realise that they can do things much faster. We can look at what we're doing adds value to our customers and the focus of the business completely changes. Happier customers, more profit and fewer bugs, what is not to like. Well, I will tell you who doesn't like it, most of your department heads. They are department heads because of the current structure in the way that you're working, if you change things, they may no longer be fit to be the department head or they may not even have a department. One educational client I had had quite buggy software and started into using Agile, with automated testing and by the end of it, we had a hundred thousand automated tests. I would not always recommend that the number of tests is the same as quality but just by the nature of the software run off a lot of variables so that meant a lot of testing. The outcome was that we got the bug rate to a position where we needed three decimal points to measure the percentage of bugs. This impacted the customer service who suddenly had fewer calls into support. to the point where it was difficult for this department head to justify having seven full-time staff to handle three calls a week. Now as it turned out there were other areas of pain that the customers were having so they redirected staff to look at those areas. Adapt or retire.

If we have created a product team that also do the day-to-day support, then the support calls go down. This means that the percentage of time available for projects increase. We get other areas of pain removed or updated, automated or whatever the appropriate solution should be. We start to form virtuous circles. Initially, the team is mainly supporting fixing bugs but by year two they are break-even and more time is spent enhancing and dealing with technical debt. The product has more features and less buggy for the customer.

Marketing

I have witnessed with my own eye's organisations take an idea, develop and test it, then somewhere in the project plan, there is a task to involve marketing or communications if it's an internal product. This is a model where we build something and hand it to the marketing department to say now go and sell this. There are a lot of successful organisations out there that manage marketing in this way, but it is not too radical a question to ask whether our marketing departments could be used earlier in the process before we have built everything.

At one level for the marketing department, things may seem very similar. We are going to have releases and we want to highlight the positive benefits for our customers through various forms of communication or advertising to maximise sales or maximise uptake of the service. You could argue that Agile with its rapid consistent delivery still falls into this model. Potentially instead of one or two big software drops per year, we may get one every month. When we look at producers like Apple, Microsoft, Google or Facebook and many others we see that they drop in new features and bug fixes regularly. This approach is no longer new or radical and is becoming mainstream within the software and web-based product marketing. Yes, this will affect your workflow, it may mean that certain skill sets need to be expanded and arguably unlike a lot of other departments, Agile for the marketing department has a reasonable case to say if we are doing more then we need more people. I will leave you to have that discussion with your CEO and you can let us know if you were successful.

We have mentioned earlier in this book that Agile is based around delivering value to customers and trying to deliver that value as soon as it is possible to do so. When we talk about testing you will see that the desire is to give good quality working software with the emphasis on working. When you are regularly dropping software updates, it can be possible to pull a feature and drop it into the next delivery if it's only two or four weeks away. When we deliver waterfall projects with a fixed budget, it means when the money runs out, we are forced to deliver whatever we have got. This can mean some features are dropped or what might appear to be working on the front screen has a small army of minions doing manual processing at the backend to compensate for the fact that some automated workflow is not fully working or even missing entirely. When you have product teams, we know we have resources to continue working on things and if it is not ready and working it goes into the next drop. Short lead times remove or greatly reduce the risk to our customers. There's going to be exceptions to this like time-bound activities such as the Olympics or a music festival.

The next question is how do we know what the customers will value? If you are delivering internally for example making a change to the company's intranet. Then we have access to our customers, they are the users of the system and their managers. It should not be too difficult to physically ask them what it is they want to see. My word of caution here is the same one I point out to analysts, on how we asked these questions. When we ask people what do you want, we may get the reply of a trip to the moon, but their more practical need may be for a mobile phone that can last the commute to work and back without needing to be charged. This is the not so subtle difference between needs and wants.

For external customers again we can ask them directly, focus groups, questionnaires and other such feedback mechanisms are well established within the IT industry across many organisations. We do have other soft data that we can look at to try and find out what are the pain points or compelling events that surround our software or the services we offer. An example I saw was with a client that had a list of features that they could potentially add to their smartphone app. This begs the question of which one should be built first. The traditional method would be to do a cost-benefit analysis and see if there was a clear winner in profitability. In this case, it wasn't clear, each of the features wherein a similar ballpark for the development costs and each saw around 3% of the customers base per year come to contact them for each item.

In Agile we would like to expand the role of Marketing to be guiding the organisation in answering these questions. It is a department after all that tries to advertise products to our customers' needs and wants. I'm not going to go into the solutions here, anybody working in a marketing department will probably without too much thought rhyme off a handful of ways that we could try and find out from our customers which of these they value the most. It is not the mechanics of how we do it, the change comes with the approach of doing it upfront. One note of caution or advice on this is that we normally think that to do something we need to take active action but there are some passive sources of information that are readily available. Many organisations completely ignore or even worse on occasions try to pretend they don't exist because they give us bad news and that is not welcome. These sources are our customer complaints and our service desk. If one of our customers has taken the time and effort to complain about something, it probably is a big enough deal for them to have taken time out of their lives to let us know their opinions. This should be seen as useful information as a product not working as expected by our customers. We could potentially be trying to address the wrong market segment where it's not the best fit and therefore gives the consumer problems. The service desk is a litany of the bugs and problems that can either be inherent in the application which is screaming out to be fixed or maybe we just have a bad interface that is not intuitive. The iPhone did not introduce any new technology into the smartphone market. There were touchscreens, applications, cameras and good quality screen resolution available in other models. What Apple does so successfully is to take what others did and make it better. Many years ago, when the iPad came out I was able to hand it to my then three-year-old son and he was able to make it work, literally an interface that a young child could understand, there's the blue button for the drawing app. The information on your service desk should be a goldmine to help you identify what's good and what's bad about our product. Please get used to looking at these types of information and use them to help the organisation to focus more on customer value. Ask yourself when you last saw the marketing manager ask for a meeting with the service desk manager to discuss any trends in service desk calls. In most organisations, this does not happen, but I would suggest to you that it should.

It is often much easier to sell things internally to those that have the power to make a change if we can back it up with some statistical evidence. I have indicated that I have a preference for evidence-based decision-making. I'll give you a marketing example. While I was working for an educational client, they had the usual cyclical issues of applications for courses and in the end, a big hit on Web services when exam results were published. We focused a lot on having the correct technology and capacity to handle sudden upticks in user access. We were generally fairly successful in getting the systems up and supplying the information to our customers. Hidden away in all this data as we published exam results every quarter was in Google analytics info that indicated that more and more of the students were accessing the result service from mobile devices. I monitored and grafted this over a period of two years, and we saw growth from around 20% to where more than 50% of the students were using a mobile device. At this point, I suggested that as mobile devices were now the preferred channel for customers, that our development focus should be directed towards a mobile app rather than web pages. This brought some interesting conversations within the organisation. I still come across even today some organisations that see mobile apps as being in some way inferior and if you need real work done then you will use a PC. Potentially, we have seen a technological milestone when Apple released the latest range of laptops powered by an M1 chip which is designed for mobile devices but is more powerful than some of the best Intel or AMD rivals. Mobile devices can sometimes be easier to use. My Apple phone allows me when ordering a pizza to pay with face recognition. To me, that is an easier process than sitting at a PC trying to remember where I left my wallet to get my card and then to read digits off the back of the card. I was also shopping and running a bit late, From the car park, I was able to order Pizza that arrived shortly after I did. For me, as the customer, my preference now is to use the mobile app.

The question about mobile or web also raised some interesting questions about demographics. The age, income or any other demographic factors you want to apply will be depending on your industry. But you will have some which are relevant to your product. I am going to take some ridiculous examples to emphasize this. Care homes normally deal with elderly customers while nursery provision in kindergartens will appeal to parents on average under the age of forty. These might sound obvious examples, but it is to make you think, what is the demographic of my product and what does that demographic own in technology terms. If I find my product is aimed at the under the thirties, then I can take a reasonable guess that the vast majority of these potential customers have a mobile device and quite possibly when it comes to browsing the web or interacting with services that are most likely going to be their main device. It may be reasonable then for us to say that if we are going to release a new feature then we're going to release it on the mobile device first. You may even be more radical and say if you can get access to the mobile device why would you waste time and money building on a web service. There was an assumption along with organisations that are slowly changing but still there that we need to have equality across all platforms. Many organisations are challenging this with where the list of features available, may differ between the web version and the phone version. It is still common that websites have more features, but I am also starting to see is in my pizza example more features via my phone on the web. If your demographics do not need a web-based service do not waste your and my time building it.

A staggered delivery with mobile android first then, iPhone, web, followed by tablet variation and finally Mac. This will also allow you to measure in real-time if our customers value it. Too often we build everything in every flavour and variation in the hope that when we launch all our customers are going to love it. What if they don't. If the feedback is bad from the first platform you can use that to inform the good and bad points that we need to change. Focus groups are really useful, however, just ask the folks at Coke how many focus groups they had about new coke or Microsoft when they introduced Windows 8. I am sure everyone assured themselves that it was a wonderful product, but the true test is if the customer will put their hand in their pocket and pay for it. Think of staggered releases as just another form of marketing. You will be able to see how many customers use it and if they don't ask them what is wrong and fix it.

I mentioned earlier that the marketing department might be one of the few departments that ask for more resources, I hope now as you can see from the above it is because we are going to be asking more questions about our customers and what they value and that may require you to have more people to answer those questions.

The Sales Team

I have worked with salespeople, and I must confess it is not my greatest talent. There's a bit of personality type which you have got, or you don't. If you haven't stop torturing yourself and find something else to do. For those that do take up this way of life like my brother-in-law, life is one continual round of selling more things than you did last quarter. If you do well you are rewarded and if you don't you will probably be let, go. It's a harsh life but can be rewarding.

I borrowed the term compelling event from salespeople, which I loosely understood to be the customer has got to want your product and generally, there is something in their personal or business life which compels them to need your product. That's not to say that salespeople wait to get phone calls from people whose houses are on fire to sell them fire extinguishers. But if the customer doesn't need what you're selling you are going to have a hard job. Agile allows you to differentiate yourself from your competitors using waterfall. Typically, I will get a sales lead or request for a proposal from one of the customers. My waterfall competitor is going to say I need time to analyse, which I want you to pay for by the way and then I'm going to take the knowledge and build you something which I will show you in six to twelve months. We also have a few milestones which you will agree to make our payments when they are completed. Even though we have delivered nothing of any real value or use there will still be stage gates that you need to fork out cash for, in the hope that in some distant future a wonderful all singing and dancing bit of software will be delivered fully working and functional out of the box, or at least that is what they tell you.

For you to be talking to the customer as a salesperson then your customer already has a compelling event. This generally means they are currently suffering some pain organisationally or are about to for example an upcoming change of legislation. I want this pain to go away so much that I'm willing to pay some money to make it go away. In the Agile world, we can say to your customer what part of this is giving you the most pain. Let's build the delivery so that we take those pain points away one at a time. This means that in a few months you will be hurting a little bit less in six months and you may not even be noticing it. Now that's a good message to give your customer. We are asking about what they value and talking to them about delivering that early. It generally also means because we have delivered some feature or functionality to the customer, we can charge them for that part and get paid early, which is music to the ears of both the finance department and the sales team. In my experience when you show the customer what you're building and talk to them they almost invariably give new suggestions or new areas of the business that this could be applied to.

The sales team initially don't have too much difference in what they doing upfront. We will still put in a proposal, get the sale confirmed and have that all-important purchase order from the customer. It is in the delivery and payment schedule that things will differ. In my 40 years of working in IT and closely working with salespeople, I have never met one yet that has asked me not to deliver so quickly and please please please if the customer asks for something extra say no. This process also builds relationships between the people delivering and the customer, it has not been uncommon in my experience for the delivery team to be invited to the customer's Christmas party.

I am not going to tell salespeople how to be salespeople. With Agile you will get much closer to your customer and remove the pain faster than your competitors. It's almost a running certainty that by this method you also have lower costs. I will leave that up to yourself and your finance department about whether you see that as a sales opportunity to offer the customers a lower price or it is seen as a way to increase profitability. It's a really simple sell, you have a problem and I'm going to make it go away faster and cheaper than the competitors. What is not to like.

For some clients, the prospect of getting part of the fix now and a bit more later is an alien concept. At this point, I normally give the hospital speech. If you are sitting in a hospital bed with a broken leg and broken arm and the doctor says, "I can only fix your broken arm at the moment, but your leg needs an operation and we cannot operate until the morning when the theatre is open". Would you say to them "no way until you can fix all my limbs, I don't want you to do anything". Most people are going to be grateful that you are doing something, okay I really would like my broken leg fixed also but if you have to start with the arm first then ok. It's better than nothing. I have never come across a customer who said to me no, we will not accept an improvement to the quality of our process. The questions are around what constitutes enough to make it worthwhile delivering. This opens a window to new marketing strategies support models and contracts. If I can get things to market quicker that changes my typical return on investment calculation. For service orientated organisations delivering a new service quicker means you can start earning revenue in three to six months rather than one to two years down the road, surely that's as good.

Empowering Teams

One of the ways we get all these good outcomes is by empowering teams. Now I must confess empowerment is a buzzword. What it should mean in business terms is we give the power to make decisions to the team. This could be as simple as what time of day they want to have a meeting or more radical things like what order will we do things, or this process is unnecessary in Agile so let us do it differently. The unfortunate truth about empowerment that I have observed in practice looks a little more like this. You are Empowered to do what you want. As long as you adhere to corporate rules and policies, and you remain within operational budgets and respect operational and supervisory roles and responsibilities. Then your change must be fully authorised and permission granted to enact the change. Even then licence to change may be conditional or have a period applied e.g., this is a pilot for 2 months with the expectation that you need to prove it conclusively worked before being able to carry on after that initial period. This often feels to the employee like you are EMPOWERED to do what you are told.

I am sure many of you that have ever been in a relationship, had a child or even just has a pet, will put their hand up to say that they understood every nuance of the relationship from the start and never tried something that did not work. You kind of look at it and say that is life. We do things and they either work or they don't. We learn from that and try to adopt the things that work and avoid the things that don't. My wife drinks coffee in the morning and tea at night. I thought for long enough that she would like tea in the morning, but I was wrong. See life and learning.

Part of the ethos of Agile is continual improvement. This means trying things out. The meeting at 10 am is poorly attended can we move it to another time. Let's try it for the next sprint and see if it makes a difference.

View the results of the change at the retrospective and decide if it worked. If it did keep it, if not try again could an alternative time around mid-day work better. There is a danger that we treat every minor change like a mini waterfall project. Analyse it to death think of every pro and con then have a big debate about whether we should adopt it. This comes from a culture when change is seldom and expected to become the new normal for a long time. In Agile our horizons are typically the next two weeks. We can try something and in such a short period it is unlikely to be disastrous to the entire organisation. There is an assumption that we will continually tinker with the process to see if we can make it better or faster. This is not restricted to the startup. I had a long-established team that decided after two years one of the columns on the sprint board was not needed.

To truly respect and empower your team, make them aware that they and not the managers are responsible for the delivery. They can decide how to organise themselves and have the ability to try new ways of doing things. My strong advice is, make the change measurable. If you cannot measure it then you cannot say if it was a success. How often have you seen on performance reviews words like improve, reduce or enhance? These are meaningless. You were late a hundred days last year but you were only late ninety-nine days this year, so you have improved. Find some way to objectively measure your change then review it, did it work?

Line Managers Take Note

Line managers generally do not have any say in what the teams do. It is no longer your tester; it is the team's tester. Different teams may do it differently. That is not a crime it is just what works best for that team. I had one team that were mainly younger men and that was happy to work later and have late meetings because most of them will still be half asleep at 8 am. Another team had older members with childcare and for them finishing up on time was a high priority so they wanted to have meetings in the mornings, That is ok the makeup of the teams and especially the tasks they are being asked to do will be different so let them find the way that works for them.

You best to get in your head that they work for the customer and team, and they are no longer under your control, despite any lines that may be drawn on a human resources chart. Think of them as having moved to a new role, not in your department, it will make the mental transition easier. Then get on to Human Resources and ask them to stop bugging you about the employees training plans it's not your bag anymore.

Corporate Tooling

The whole company using the same tools set has many appeals from cost savings to minimising support. What is not good is being handed a spade and being told to paint the fence. The toolset needs to be fit for the job your team is doing. If it is not them dump it. Classically waterfall testing round 1, round 2 the UAT approach does not work for Agile.

The other danger is some overzealous admin thinking what a good job they are doing by standardising the configuration of software. This is a straight jacket to the team. If one team want 20 statuses for their delivery and another want 3 then let them do what is best for their team.

I don't like to speak ill of the dead, but enterprise project management software is pointless in an Agile world. Please do not throw your waterfall bureaucracy anywhere near an Agile team. If you buy a horse feed it hay if you buy a car, feed it petrol. Do not ever try to shoehorn an Agile development into software not designed for Agile. And by that, I do not mean that it has a section thrown in called Agile. I once saw a car that could be converted into a boat. The extra weight of the boat component made it poor to drive and the extra bulk and size of the car made it bad for stability, speed and steering as a boat. Try to pick something that was designed for Agile there are only really five or so on the market use one of them, not a bolt on to something called Agile. It is better to use post-it notes on the wall than use a waterfall tool. Let us be honest with ourselves most enterprise project management is focused on the costs and charges to the correct budget, it is not there to plan anything.

Remember standardised tooling assumes that we are all doing the same thing in the same way. The mere fact that you are doing Agile means you are not doing the same thing in the same way, so it is unlikely to work.

Finance & Project Management Office

I am a part-qualified accountant, I have run my own business and for three years working with an organisation that trains accountants. I have a degree in Economics and Business Administration as well as forty years working in multiple industries and countries around the world. Therefore, I will contend with you that I have a strong enough background and knowledge to speak about finance. I think that many of the values of the finance department are worthy, but I will argue that what is best for the finance department is not necessarily in all cases best for the business or our customers. Let me elaborate.

Our purpose in life is to facilitate the smooth running of the organisation and provide governance of the process. I accept that there needs to be governance and as a project manager you do not want me to buy myself a Ferrari out of the project budget. Here is an interesting question for you. I have done this calculation on several organisations and when I add up the cost of software licences for SAP or Oracle then add in the hardware and the teams that are needed to support it. Then also add the cost of the finance department and a little overhead for the general business that need to approve purchase orders and process goods receipt notes I come up with a calculation of around $150-200 for each purchase order. Could you explain why we should justify this cost? A $10 item costs me $160 minimum to buy. How does that serve the organisation?

My next challenge is based on decades of experience of working with finance departments and their surrogates in the project management office,

I have had numerous discussions with finance departments over project spend profiles. In an ideal world 25% of the way through the project I will have spent 25% of the budget. Very few IT projects follow this ideal spend profile. Most commonly this is focused on the infrastructure spend. Some projects need to buy all the infrastructure upfront, and others will build a pilot as a proof of concept and then expand out the infrastructure towards the end of the project. There will be variations if you're using third parties because there is a lag usually between when the work is done when it is invoiced and finally paid. We can smooth some of that out with accruals. Part of the finance role should be to look at this project spend and highlight if there was not a good reason for either an underspend which could indicate that we're not delivering or the alternative an overspend which could indicate that the project is going to go over budget. One of the questions I never get asked is if I am delivering good quality software. Quality is not a direct deliverable of the finance department. I can deliver a pile of stinking poo, but it will be considered a successful project if it is within budget and on time.

Over the decades, I have only ever had one project that I cancelled voluntarily. I inherited a small project from another project manager. It was one of those classic road crashes, the business wanted to automate a process that would save them £150,000 per year. The current project spent was around £350,000 and I was informed by the third party supplier delivering this, it was going to cost a further £250,000 to complete but with no guarantee that the system there were going to put in place had the correct capacity for the throughput that we wanted. If it underperformed, we may need to throw more equipment at it and this would potentially cost even more. This particular business worked on a return of investment of three years. To my accountancy brain, I calculated that this project could not return the value or breakeven, therefore I proposed that we should can this project. Ironically while the business and IT were convinced with my cost assessment it was the finance department that was most concerned. What transpired was that this large multinational company did not have a working process for cancelling projects. It wasn't that in principle or theory they didn't allow for projects to be cancelled, it was more the nuts and bolts of which contra entries, where do you allocate any unused budget et cetera. This indicated to me and subsequently borne out by many decades of delivery that finance departments do not generally cancel projects. In fairness to the finance department, they could argue that it is not our role to cancel projects that should be the responsibility of the team managing the project or another part of the organisation. We effectively just handle the money and tell you when it is spent, our role is to facilitate your purchases and make payments. You can make a reasonable case that this all sounds justifiable. I want my facilities department to keep the heating and light on I don't expect them to be responsible for what I do within the building that they are heating and lighting, they are just facilitating the ability to work in the office.

If you take the role of a facilitator then fine, stand back and hand over the pot of money leaving the control for the spend to the project team. However, the reality is that the CEO can grant me several million dollars as a project or programme manager. I can have an agreement from my technical teams and business users to spend some of that money, but I cannot spend a penny unless I use the finance departments process. For most organisations, the process of ordering an office chair by the department head is the same process that is applied to a project. I will give you this ridiculous example. I was given a project with €14.5 million spend and appointed the project manager to spend it. Within the finance application, my role as a project manager was limited to spending €1200 without escalating approval processes. When I was ordering a lot of hardware in the region of €400K it required me to go up the food chain all the way to the VP. That would be the same vice president who had approved the budget for me to spend. Whenever we see duplication of effort it must indicate that as an organisation, we are wasting money. It also indicates that despite what the board of directors wants, and the project was to deliver for the business they are not authorised to do so by the finance processes. If you're only going to take one thing away from this section, please consider whether you should amend your processes for projects. I know one size fits all makes life easier for yourself as a facilitator your point of existence is not to make life easier for yourself.

Here are another couple of tales from the trenches. I was working for a client on a series of acquisitions and another very small one came along that was an office with a few staff. The question was could I pick it up along with the other stuff I was doing. I looked at it and estimated that it would take two to three days of my time over three months and came to the conclusion it was possible and started to work on it. It then transpired that this really little one was for a different part of the business and used a different budget code. Therefore, I could not charge to that part of the business. I was asked to hand it over by this time 50% complete and a brand new budget code and the project was kicked off in the other area of the business. I think this is a prime example of where the finance systems get in the way of common sense and waste a lot of money, by the way, the systems are supposed to be there to control spend not cause it.

Another one was when I inherited a project from another project manager who had left the organisation. It was the start of the new financial year. The budget for the previous year had not been fully spent as the order for the hardware had been delayed while there was a decision about which data centre to install it in. The finance department had absorbed the unspent budget and not allocated it to the following year. There was a process that appeared to resemble what happens at school when you need a letter from your parents to be excused from class to attend a dentist appointment. My previous colleague had not done this. When I pointed out that it was silly to assume I could deliver this project without the servers I was told that I would need to raise a change control and argue the case to have an additional budget allocated for this year. Now I am not wanting to decry the previous PM, but we need to get into our head that projects do not care about financial years and you giving me your problem is not on. We need to be a bit more grown-up in our conversations. Our customers do not care about when we decide to declare our financial year, the colleague on the customer service desk has little or no care. Also, the person installing hardware in a data centre wants to ensure the cabling is correct not which arbitrary day it happens to land. The finance department needs to handle any issues with end of years or end of quarters as an internal finance department issue and not inflict it on the rest of the business that is too busy delivering to the customer. I would suggest that the first change is that any unspent budget in a project automatically rolls over to the next year. The assumption should be that if it is needed that need is not magically going to disappear because it is now the 1st of April.

Now let's look at her Agile can change things. What is it going to look like as a staffing profile if we pull a team together and intend to keep that team there for the full duration of the project? For most weeks or months my staffing profile can effectively be looked at as a fixed cost for the core team. This indicates that reporting the same thing week after week is ever so slightly pointless and for this reason, you should consider having one reporting structure for waterfall projects and another reporting structure for Agile projects.

Some organisations also impose quality checks as part of the authorisation to open a budget code for a project. Here again if one of your quality measures is that we have a project plan then you're not going to get it from Agile because they don't use them. Again, the financial stage gates need to be tailored one for waterfall and one for Agile. This goes back to a subject we highlighted earlier that change means that things are going to have to change. And that equally applies to the finance department. A simpler reporting framework will inevitably mean less work for the finance department. Any department, as I'm sure finance is aware when it is overstaffed for the workload, it either needs to find additional work which gives value to the business or reduce staff numbers to more appropriate levels. I would argue in my experience that in most organisations it takes five to ten days to initiate budget codes. Therefore, the business and project team sit in a holding pattern waiting to kick things off fully until the finance department initiates the codes which are needed in timesheet systems, ERP and any other number of downstream applications. It may be a justifiable use of the additional staff hours available, to reduce the time to process requests.

One of the items that have always puzzled me is that I can take a business case to a board and get their approval, but when I come to get a budget code it needs to go up the food chain to be re-approved again. Can the finance department figure out some way to know what the board have approved and not reinvent it? When I approached one finance department with my request to have a budget code allocated to my new project, I was informed that it required to be authorised. I informed the person that it had been at the board the previous day, only to be informed that it had not been approved to finance and they would need to get authorisation from the same people that had just approved it the day before. I need to challenge this if you have any processes that you are the gatekeepers for then it is you and not the person requesting it that needs to be informed of board decisions.

There is another way to manage projects and that is to get rid of them. One of the incentives to have projects is that in many countries they allow tax write-offs against capital expenditure. By instituting a project, it becomes administratively easier for the finance department to identify the spend. In essence, all that is happening is that the costs are assigned to a budget code which is identified as capital expenditure. There are lots of ways of assigning money to a budget code that does not involve projects. We do this all the time for departmental spending. So that begs the question if we want to allocate some expenditure to a budget code do, we need to spend 10 to 25% of that said budget to make it happen. Probably the answer is no. The tester that fills in the timesheet at the end of the week is quite capable of selecting the appropriate capital allocated budget code and the project manager when ordering equipment can equally assign the appropriate code at the time of raising the purchase order.

As a side note, most of the large ERP systems which are on the market today were initially designed for manufacturing businesses and have a particular ethos built into them which revolves around stock ordering production and distribution. If in life you and your partner have three kids, but you buy a two-seater sports car then do not be surprised if it isn't quite designed for your family needs. Equally, if you are in a manufacturing industry then ERP systems may be ideal for you. There are a lot of businesses out there that are not manufacturing, and it imposes crippling processes on the business to try and make the business fit the software. This never works out well, please recognise that and stop building processes that fit the software rather than the business.

It is possible to run Agile oriented projects with traditional project codes and this is done in many places daily. This does not mean that it is the optimal solution. Just as I mentioned about having to fit your processes to suit software it is equally not a good idea to run your software development to suit the financial system. The best way of doing it is to form product teams. A team of resources that have the skills to maintain and make any improvements to the software. They will get more efficient the longer we keep them together. Therefore, within reason, we want to keep that team together and stable. Imagine if you will that you have a support team for a particular application or set of applications and we increase the headcount by 30%. This team now can conduct 30% of its annual resources to be dedicated to delivering project work. Their spending on project work is recorded in the timesheet and allocated to the appropriate project budget and capitalised. It is a really simple model and probably exist somewhere in your organisation right now. So were going to build teams to support things and deliver projects because they will be the best people to deliver the projects as they already know the product. The organisation will gain from the efficiencies and deliver faster and cheaper costs. The rest of the organisation will want to move forward with this approach because it is very hard to tell your CEO "Yes we could deliver this six months quicker and be 40% cheaper but the financial system will not support it, therefore you are just going to have to pay more and accept it is delivered later". As a finance department, you will have to adapt, the good news is we don't need all the extra bureaucracy of projects to do it.

I accept that we will not always be able to fill all positions internally. The time to recruit or lack of technical expertise in some areas will require us to bring in freelance contractors. Having been on the receiving end of this process many many times I have a small observation that I think highlights where finance processes overrule the desire of the delivery. I was working on a project that had a two-year delivery and was initially brought in on a six-month contract. When the time for renewal came along and everyone appeared happy for me to continue in the role. I was advised that I could only get a further six-month extension, not for any business or technical reason. This was related to finance processes. A purchase order over a certain value needed to be approved at a much higher level. So, the solution is to create lots of smaller purchase orders so that we can keep within budget authorisation. I am a person who is not afraid to ask why, and the basic response was it is technically possible but they do not like to bother people very high up as it tends to get them to ask questions about what they are signing off.

This to me appears to be a troublesome approach to try and keep things under the radar. If a normal line manager did this kind of thing ordering new desks for their team five at a time, they would be brought to task for trying to go under the radar. This is the Indian cobra problem again. We introduce unwanted behaviours into the organisation by applying arbitrary rules based on the software. It is possible to have multiple approval levels based on role or budget codes, the main reason this facility is not used very often is that it has an overhead for the finance department. Potentially some of the time saved on reporting could be dedicated to enabling this flexibility into the organisation to meet the business need. Now, this is not just theoretical I have had any number of freelance contractors walk out of projects in mid-stream because their time-limited contracts had ended, and they had a better offer on the table. This is all fair and I have no problem with this. If I employ someone on a project and they do the work, then I cannot complain if they do not accept the offer of an extension. The problem comes that the reason the extension was needed in the first place was that someone in the finance department did not want to walk up to a VP or director and ask them to sign a bit of paper.

I have included the project management office or PMO as it is sometimes shortened to because while the reason for its existence is supposed to be the delivery of quality and financial controls my experiences that 80 to 90% of the focus is on finance. Risks and issues are required to be tracked but the main focus for the PMO is any financial implications resulting from these risks or issues. This close tie and focus on finance is the reason that I have lumped in the PMO with the finance department because in most cases they appear to be joined at the hip.

When we introduce Agile, we replace some of the traditional waterfall products and artefacts with alternatives. In theory, it is straightforward, for example, project plans are replaced with a prioritised backlog, checkpoint reports on progress are replaced with an Agile board which is real-time and if somebody higher up wants to know how the project is doing send the

URL to the board, issue logs are replaced with blocked cards. The team will not maintain a risk log because technical risks are assessed in real-time as part of the sprint planning process. High-level testing strategy plans at the beginning are replaced with sprint plans. There are many more examples that we could look at, but this should be enough of a list for you to make a start.

The reason I phrase this in this manner is to indicate to you that when we say that we do not have a project plan it is not something to panic about. Within Agile there are alternative ways of capturing this information. Taking story points as an example, these enable us to give real-time information about the progress on delivery. I will tell you one of my apocryphal stories as a waterfall project manager. I was doing my usual rounds of the teams checking up on progress to update my Microsoft project plan. I asked one colleague how things were going, and I was advised they were 20% of the way through the delivery which was okay because we were at the start of the project. However, I pointed out that in last week's report he had advised me that he was 25% of the way through. This made me enquire whether the scope of what he was doing had in some way increased, which would explain the lower percentage. The answer I got was quite enlightening "okay then stick me down for 30%". That one encounter highlighted something to me which was of key importance when you see all these wonderful reports with percentages filled in on some bar chart it is either based on a flawed assumption that 50% of the time means 50% done or as in the case above is based on a hunch. Agile by using story points can give quantifiable numerical testable results. 300 points in the backlog to deliver with 211 done, I know exactly how far through the deliveries we are and exactly how much we've got to do.

I have a section of my book on how your brain works at work that goes through estimation and explains why our quantitative measurements are so widely out. Traditional methods of estimating the time of delivery are 50-

200% inaccurate, Agile has its own level of inaccuracy from estimation but it's in the range of 15-30%. Therefore, proven empirically time and time again I can rely on Agile estimates with a greater degree of certainty when comparative estimation is used.

When we deliver in little chunks, we are going to find issues problems, blockers, technical difficulties, lack of infrastructure or internal expertise. Whether in waterfall or Agile, it's just that with Agile we are going to make it visible and you can find out earlier. Do not worry about this, it is a good thing. If we have a problem, I want to learn about it as soon as possible to give me as much time as I can have to get it fixed.

My advice is to create a table with all the items that you use for controls. Project plans, checkpoint reports, Financial reports, et cetera et cetera. In one column you will put a tick or cross if it is appropriate to waterfall and in the next, you will put a tick or cross if it is appropriate to Agile. Then you will add all the Agile artefacts like a backlog, blocker list et cetera et cetera and tick or cross which are appropriate for waterfall and Agile as you did with the list above. Please do not do this in isolation, talk to either the Agile coach or the teams delivering. Now you have a two-stream process, apply as appropriate.

There is a principle in Agile that even if you are just working with post-it notes stuck on the office wall that the progress is visible. If I want to know whether the company logo has been replaced on the website there is a card for it and it is either going to be in a backlog, doing or done. If it is important enough to me, I will go and have a look for myself. For a few of my clients that were using JIRA and Confluence, which are very common products in the industry. I have asked what are the KPIs they want to see. I then created a report either in JIRA or Confluence which updates with real-time information every time you open the page. My weekly reporting consisted of a URL. Anyone wanting to see the progress could link to the URL whenever they wanted. There is a practical reason for this when Agile teams are dealing with a blocker, they will move heaven and earth to get that block removed. When teams are meeting daily to give progress checks at the stand-up then things literally change from day to day. As we are working to a two week timescale then the items, we are working on are going to be generally small incremental changes to what we had the last time. This in turn means they are going to go across the board quickly getting developed and tested and put into the done pile within those two weeks. Compared to the speed of progress when we roll anything up in a waterfall project this is the difference between a sports car and a tractor. In practice, any report older than 12 hours is old news.

I'll give you a working example of this. I was asked to do a classic checkpoint report weekly to be delivered to the PMO by noon on a Monday. It highlighted that we had a problem that we were blocked because we needed an account to connect to another server, we had requested it from the team's manager, but hadn't got it and it was holding us up. On a Monday morning, the PMO collected my report along with many others and produced a program deck. The slide deck was issued at the end of Thursday for a review meeting the following Monday. As my report had a high impact issue, I was invited to the Monday meeting to explain what the impact would be on the project deliveries. At the meeting, I informed the group that we had received the password two hours after the report was submitted and we had not only completed the work and tested it, but it had gone live on Sunday. After this happened several times it became clear I was wasting my time and theirs. This is where we decided to come up with real-time reporting rather than historical reporting. Remember anything older than twelve hours is old news in Agile.

This brings up an important part about timescales. In Agile they can be a lifetime. Any process or procedure that you have which takes more than 40 hours to complete is potentially going to be a blocker for Agile. Just as we highlighted with the finance department the software delivery should not have to be adapted to PMO processes. Each team will have different deliveries and a different structure. So, there is no one size fits all. Comments like "this is our process" or "this is how we do things" are archaic terms. The assumption is that we will be the same yesterday today and tomorrow and the day after that. Increasingly with business and with customer expectations, there is a reasonable question for them to ask if I can order a book ten o'clock at night and is delivered by Amazon the next morning why it took five days to get something out of the PMO. The PMO often has a governance role in signing off those things that are good to proceed to go live. In the next section, I going to touch on change control management, and I would advise you to read that section also because it also applies to the PMO.

Change And Risk Management

Change management is great, I want things to be known about, assessed for risk. When things go wrong it is really good to have a backout plan. If I am going to impact any services or even bring them down, then people need to know. All these statements I have absolutely no problem with.

Now let me give you an example of a very IT savvy business I worked with. The process runs as follows, all code changes need to be in for four PM and committed. At five PM the builds will kick-off. Between six o'clock and midnight a series of automated tests will be run. At 10 AM the following morning the test results will be examined. If the software has passed the tests, it is put live at 2 PM.

This is not a fantasy scenario it is one I worked in. Ironically, they wanted to bring Agile into this organisation because the software development was running so much slower than the infrastructure capabilities. Consider your change processes. I would not be surprised if by a given date change requests need to be filed either on paper or electronically or both. Explicit approval needs to be sought from business and technical people and only then will be put forward to some form of Change Advisory Board, or CAB as it is normally known as. Some organisations even split the CABs with an initial technical CAB being held one or two days before the general CAB. It is not unusual to have some kind of time delay between approval and implementation. If you are lucky, you will get through all that in a week if you are unlucky, it will be ten to fourteen days. We can process things quicker, but these are generally reserved for emergency CABs and conducted when something is broken, and we need to put in a fix rapidly. But that is seen very much as an exception and not to be encouraged.

The challenge is simple, the software can be developed and tested deployed in twelve to sixteen hours, rather than asking Agile teams to please sit on their hands for a week or two while you email out CAB papers. Ask yourself what we need to do as an organisation to get a fit for purpose change control process. Review your change control procedure and start thinking about how to reduce your timescales. A very simple method to speed things up is to pull rather than push information to the CAB members. Normally the assumption is that nobody can assess what changes or ask questions unless they are physically there at the meeting at two o'clock on a Wednesday. I have spent many boring hours of my life listening to what other people are going to do in different divisions of an organisation waiting for my change to come up as number 23 on the agenda. I introduced an interesting approach where all the changes were made available via a website and it was up to the individual members to review them. It changed from I need explicit consent to nobody has objected. I heard all kinds of mumbling about how this would be the end of the world and catastrophe would be just around the corner. Despite the protestations, it worked just fine. If nobody objected to a change within the allotted time it was deemed to be automatically approved and could be scheduled for delivery. All are the ones where anybody highlighted a concern or had not had a question answered were tabled for discussion at the cab meeting. Some claimed that they may not have time to review the appropriate changes before they were automatically approved. My response to this was a little bit harsh, if you are not competent or able to do your job then maybe that is what you should address, rather than the change to the process. As a rule, I do try and avoid making this personal but, in this case, it needed to be addressed. The result was the complainers stopped complaining. The duration of the CAB meeting was cut in half and on average this knocked two days off the change control process. This touches on another area called cycle time used in some forms of Agile. You look at the processing in terms of what are the blocking points and how we can try to either remove them or reduce them. I give this example to show that there are ways of still maintaining scrutiny and letting people have their say about changes without it being a long-winded process taking up a lot of time and holding up deliveries.

Give yourself the challenge to see what we need to do as a start, to change your processes so that someone can come up with a change on Monday morning and we can implement it on Friday afternoon. This should just be a starting point; we want to get to the position where it is normal that we can turn things around in 12 hours. This could mean that you have to put challenges forward to other parts of the organisation. For example, the testing department. Rather than producing a test report, which is normally generated out of some other electronic system, can we just get access to the electronic system to see all the tests are passed?

This touches on a general point that I hinted at above when I talked about financial reporting in Jira. A lot of the reports that we produce manually usually are just simply extracted from other places. It takes time to take the information out, format it, update to the latest version for this week and finally send out an email or put it in a file share somewhere. Every time you do a task that is copy and paste ask yourself how much value that exercise has and would it not be possible for the consumer of the data to look at the source system just as you are. I have been in some places where I was informed that the line manager likes it that way and therefore the team need to present the data in that particular format. My challenge to that is if one of his employees decided not to do what the line manager asked because the employee did not like it that way with the line manager be okay with that.

It used to be the case that to get information from systems needed specialist DBAs with SQL skills and access to the core systems to run and extract detailed exports of which the outputs were often just text files containing strings of data. Managers could rightly turn round and say there is no way I can read a comma-separated value file please put it into a humanly readable format. We got used to the idea that we need to extract data and reformat it. There is nothing wrong with this the only problem is that technology has moved on in the last 20 years. In virtually every application you have, it is either available on your mobile phone or as a URL that you can go and look at the same information yourself. By producing reports, we are manually cranking out things to solve a problem that disappeared 20 years ago.

I did a back of a cigarette packet calculation for one government department that I was working with, and I came up with a figure of 11% of the work of that department involved copying data from one place to another. If we were to look at the PMO it may well, go up to 60%. This is wasteful to the organisation to get your managers or those that need to read the data trained on how to get the info for themselves or produce automated reporting. Do not throw away 11% of your organisation's human resources because the managers do not want to learn or are too lazy to do it for themselves.

As an experiment once while in the role of a delivery manager I logged that we were producing over seventy reports per week. I decided not to send them out one week. This is a "let's see who screams" test. Of the seventy reports only three were chased up that week and a further six by month-end, those nine reports I kept and the rest were dumped. Try it yourself I suspect you will get similar results

There is a real-world cost for this to projects. The projects will often talk about the burn rate, that is the money the project spends per day on resources. A not too unusual example may be a team of ten with an average cost of $500 giving me a burn rate of $5000 a day. This is a real cost to the business and each day we have to extend the project timelines will cost us $5000. If the project ultimately has to be extended by another month, then the calculation is really simple 20 working days times $5000 equals $100,000. That is real cash going out of the business. I'm not trying to imply that the change management process is directly responsible for $100,000 for every project but it has to accept that part of this can be due to delays with change management. Even if the process is just inefficient that will have a real cost to the business.

I have had it retorted that it is not the change process that is the problem it is the fact that projects are not organised and do not put in change requests with enough time to be processed. I would see this as a legitimate call in some cases. Over the years I have connected any number of offices and manufacturing buildings. It is almost like a shopping list, I know I'm going to need a WAN connection, I know I'm going to need LAN network and wireless within the building and that will require a proportionate number of routers and network switches we have done it before, it's repeatable and we should have a good idea of what is expected and be able to put our change controls in on time.

Historically change management developed out of IT and operations departments who are people who have mainly focused on IT infrastructure. Therefore, it is not too surprising that the processes that were developed in the main revolved around infrastructure. It is slightly different when we talk about software. This is because we are often doing something new. By the nature of doing new things, we do not have the benefit of hindsight to give us our shopping list of things to do. I do not have sympathy for projects that say we were going to set up a website, but we didn't remember that we needed a connection to the Web server through the firewall. However, can anybody tell me what ports need to be open to allow for the next generation of iPad devices to talk to Oracle backend two versions from now? My networking and security colleagues would rightly say that we need to see the specifications, if not published it would be unrealistic for them to make predictions if they haven't done it before. When you move house, you have still got to go to work and something like Google maps or our local geographical knowledge may enable you to make a rough prediction about what your daily commute time maybe. I once started a new contract and intended to travel by car. What I hadn't factored in was that major roadworks were happening on my route. This resulted in me choosing to take the train which in theory was slower but in practice because of the roadworks was a quicker option. When we build software, we may also fall into similar issues. The original intention was to do a process in a particular way, but we find out that it is too slow and we try a different method. This is perfectly normal and in development, we try a prototype of the code then attempt to scale up and if it doesn't work, we will change.

Within Agile an added complication of the way of working is that we break the work down into small chunks. Monday morning to build a prototype, towards the middle or the end of that week will do a test run around connectivity and data flows. All being well following Monday or Tuesday it's finished off and handed to the testers. Again, assuming that the testing is complete the software will be packaged up at the end of week two and it's ready to deploy. If you're going to work in this manner, there is no place for change control processes that take up to two weeks. Where we de-risk the process is simple. If some of the code does not work or is not signed off by the customer, it does not go into the build. I demo my latest changes to the customer towards the end of the sprint and they say, "I like items one and two but I am not so sure about that new interface now that I see it, I think we should go back to the old interface". So, for my change control to be published well in advance I need to be a clairvoyant and predict the future. I should have known the customer was going to change their mind about the look of the interface on item three and not included it in my change control. Alternatively, I should wait until after the demo and then deploy one to two weeks later. I will counter that the software is good, Items one and two will be added to the code base and item three will get reworked and be in the next sprint. I now have a live version, a pre-live ready to go and waiting on the change process and the next version starting on Monday. We now need to store the pre-live version somewhere, ok let's build another environment, that costs money and needs time to manage but its ok everyone will understand that we have to spend another $50,000 because we cannot possibly turn around changes in just a couple of days let alone hours.

My challenge here is the same as a challenge I gave to the finance department, you need to design a process that is fit for purpose. We know that we can approve changes within a day when we need to, they are called emergency changes. In the process procedure, all the structural requirements are there we just deliberately choose not to use them. So, here's a challenge what in your processes do you need to do to turn that around that you remove the word emergency and replace it with normal. Can you please tell me what law of nature would prevent a daily thirty-minute CAB meeting to review changes submitted the previous day? I don't think you will find one. If cost is your worry be reassured whatever the cost of your thirty-minute meeting is I would bet that it is less than my projects $5000 burn rate.

There is a form of Agile where we will look at the cycle time, that being the time it takes from start to finish of a process. We look at each part of the process and ask is it still relevant or does it exist as some archaic throwback to a problem that no longer exists anymore. Next, we want to look at what value each part gives us and if it cannot demonstrate clear value then it is a candidate to be dropped. What is left is probably important and the next challenge is how can we do it as quickly as possible. I have worked on quite many mergers and acquisitions and for the company on the receiving end of the acquisition, it is not unusual to be told that you need to adopt some new process. This is a gun at your head scenario. You do not have the usual grounds to try and argue, "but we really need this honest". You just get told that you need to do it. If you are in that situation and I asked you to dock 50% off the time of your change control process or you are going to be fired. Then I think you would come up with some inventive and interesting ways to make sure that the process ran more quickly. Ah! but is this not riskier I imagine the reader thinking. This will lead us on to risk management.

When you try to manage risk in an organisation, you are trying to prevent harm to ourselves. We may talk about the customers but the thing that we worry about the customers is that they may not buy our product which harms ourselves. Everything inherently has risk, but the duration that you are exposed to that risk multiplies the effect. If I launch a new phone or car each year onto the market and it does not work, then I'm exposed to that risk for an entire year until the new model can be delivered. This may sound like an extreme case, but it just emphasises long delivery times lead to long exposure to risks. Let us look at the other extreme if I'm able to turn software around and get it tested and out the door and 12 hours then my risk is down to what can happen in 12 hours. Ah, I hear you again saying that even exposure for 12 hours to a risk of some flaw in a bit of software may be unacceptable.

When challenged by such an approach one of the first things I ask is what is the service level agreement for this service. Some are seen as very high priority and may have a fixed time of four hours. Others are deemed less important and will have a recovery time objective as the jargon describes it as 24-48 hours and in some cases at the far end of a week. Then I also enquire what is the disaster recovery profile for the service. Normally in these cases, the figures tend to go into days rather than hours. This brings up an interesting question about our perceived risk. We will build into our support models a situation where we accept that an entire service to our customers can be unavailable for two days and that it was okay because that's a service level agreement we have signed up to. However, when we start to talk about the software running on that service we appear to worry if one in a thousand customers may see a screen flicker. These two statements do not add up. If the perfection of your system is so important then upgrade the service level to the appropriate level. It is illogical to say that a screen flicker is important but is ok for the entire service to be on its knees giving a 501 error to the customer.

I am not asking for bad software to be given a free pass, but it would be logical to provide a consistent view of what the real importance of a system is. I think it is reasonable to argue a case that we consider a system to be low enough priority that we will allow the system to be completely out of service for four days before bringing it back up. Then this should be associated with the level of risk that we are willing to accept on the service whether that is software or hardware related. As long as we can deliver a software fix in the duration of the SLA for the hardware then what is the problem. If that is not the case, then you have the wrong SLAs.

I am risk-averse and that is one reason I like Agile. By adding small incremental changes onto a system and deploying these as they are ready, when it comes around to the next release, I know that I am building on a stable platform or if we have found something it will be fixed in the next release or sooner if needed. I have no problem with risk management, and I am a great believer in defence of coding which is a practice of assuming the systems we connect to may not always be there or the customer will not follow the exact process as we imagine it and are likely to press the back button. We should build our system to have that resilience and be able to handle these events. I am going to give you an example of a deployment that highlighted to me the irrational view we sometimes have of software over hardware.

I saw the system had a bug in every 10,000th customer who dropped the connection and had to press the refresh button in the browser. This was an intermittent problem, a real pain to track down and find out what it was. It turned out when we had more data than it was a capacity issue with a firewall. The fix was to purchase additional licence capacity for the firewall, but it would take about two weeks for the order and get the licences applied.

We raised this at the CAB and explained that it was still awaiting the new licences, but the customer could continue after a refresh and close the transaction. I left it at the mercy of the CAB, and I was prepared either way for the go or no go. There was the opinion that as it appeared randomly, and the customer could complete the transaction they would allow it to be deployed. Then on the morning of the release, there was a panic, and we were asked to attend an emergency meeting. There appeared to have been found a page on the site that had two full stops at the end of a sentence, and this had been missed. I thought to myself well this will be an easy fix, but the process of the organisation was that if any part of the code was changed it would need to go back through the testing cycle. I, therefore, said that the page in question was on a page that was only relevant to a particular cohort of customers and from our customer base that would be one out of every thirty thousand and as the item was not functional in nature, we would propose to leave it and pick it up in the next deployment in two weeks. I got a lot of resistance on this one until I pointed out that two days ago, they had approved something that affects every $10,000^{th}$ customer and that required the interaction of the customer to refresh the web browser. but here we have something which would affect every $30,000^{th}$ customer and probably not be noticed by the majority of them and suddenly this was more important. My point here is to be consistent, if you are going to pull the release then do it for both reasons or let it go consistently.

It is natural that for the first few Agile deployments the organisation is wary, but it soon gets normal, and the risk is seen for what it is. It is an unfortunate reality that anything made by humans can break, what is generally to most of us the important thing in our lives when our phone is broken is how long will it be until we can get it fixed.

No CEO has ever asked me for a perfect product because it would cost too much, what I and asked for is fit for purpose. The process of small incremental improvements to our software reduces the risk and the time of exposure to any potential risk. Therefore, if Agile is less risky, then it should be treated as such in the change and risk management processes. It is possible to adopt a two-stream approach and consider that adding two dropdowns to a web page and creating an automated acknowledgement email, which may be a typical bit of functionality released as part of an Agile drop, bares far less risk than a waterfall project where we have been building this thing out for months if not years and want to drop the whole thing as a fully functioning all singing and dancing release to the world. It does not make sense to apply the same change and risk management approach to both items. Please get away from one size fits all and start thinking about what is fit for purpose for each approach.

Service Management, Operational Support

All right someone has built all the stuff and it has now landed on your doorstep to try maintaining and fix. In the classic waterfall approach, the team will be highly motivated for a week or so to see the new baby in operation. Usually, by the time, we get to ten days the project is getting ready to have its farewell party and all the project teams will be going off into the sunset. If you're lucky you will just keep ticking along and it will not give you too many problems but there are some which are real stinkers and keep failing regularly possibly due to transaction volumes or some process that runs at various intervals. You will take the calls, create tickets, pass them to support teams and hopefully close them within an SLA. There's pretty much nothing you can do about it if you are handed a lemon. If you get a hundred calls a month because some part of the process doesn't work, then you're just going to have to live with the fact that you got an extra hundred calls a month. For most service management professionals handling these additional calls is a challenge in terms of meeting the service level and having the resources at the right time to answer the calls. You have no way of getting it fixed and you just have to live with it.

If on the other hand we are delivering in Agile and we find a problem with the latest release, then you can raise it with the Agile team, and they can fix it for the next release. You can even take existing problems that you have with the software and ask for them to be fixed while we are developing the new features. In Agile we want to deliver good quality working software with an emphasis on the working. If some feature of the software does not pass the tests, then it will not be in the latest release.

Therefore, we avoid passing on risk to the support teams and our customers. Agile with only a few rare exceptions will ever deploy software that is not fully working. I accept that there is an overhead that two weeks ago we could not take credit card payments and now we can. In a further four weeks will be able to take Apple Pay payments. The software that you are supporting will keep changing and not just every six months or a couple of years but on a very regular basis.

This tends to lend support organisations away from documents based on signed off copies. You know the kind of thing I'm talking about when it says not valid if printed off, the kind of thing that we get in electronic document management systems. The problem for the systems is a similar one that we addressed with ERP systems. They were designed for something different than what we want to use them for. They are designed for storing one-off documents and associating them with a customer. The document is not intended to change and can be things like a loan agreement. We want to be able to tie this document back to the customer and are very good at doing these types of things. They are also very good at giving an audit trail of who added or deleted the document. When making system documentation there is a temptation to think we have a document repository let's put it there. But it is not designed for documents that are going to be changed regularly so I would suggest possibly the wrong place to be storing your support documentation.

When we have regular incremental changes to our software support documentation needs to reflect that, and that is why many are Agile support organisations are adopting "living documentation". This is where the support document is rendered as a web page and like other web pages, we expect that when we click on the webpage it's going to give us the latest information. If you have some form of electronic knowledge base you will recognise that while we have a repository of knowledge which could be in the form of word documents or some similar format the emphasis is on finding the latest information not controlling the information audit. Some organisations may have customer information FAQs or the like when you make a change, we should expect that these are also updated with the appropriate information, possible changes to URLs and the like. The updating of these can even become a task within the Agile release. When using living documentation and we review a webpage that page as the latest info. Most and I will give the example of confluence having a full audit trail where you can go back and see all the various changes that have happened.

If your organisation adopts product teams then this will be a more radical change for you because it not only affects the frequency with which things are deployed it also affects the teams. A classic, as originally envisaged DevOps team (not the IT let's play with lots of toys type of dev-ops team that we have in many organisations) was an interesting concept. About 35 years ago people like myself who were supporting customers and internal users got fed up with software getting thrown over the fence and quite frankly not working. The support teams had to run around trying to mend or adapt things and in those days, you may have had a developer hand you a floppy disk and say there's your fix now implement it on 300 PCs, which was certainly not an easy task. So those brave souls attempted to think that development and operations could be combined. Given the name Dev for development and Ops for operations, it argued that at least some of the development effort should be focused on operational support. In my case, I wasn't totally successful, but I did get the acceptance of hyper care periods and eventually a proportion of a few developers time for what they determined the break-fix stuff. This wasn't seen as being sexy stuff and was not popular amongst the developers and the IT staff for whom a number of them lacked social skills found the concept of talking to developers quite alien. I was able to prevail with this and we pulled together support teams which included the developers and later testing effort. This is a true DevOps team. They are assigned an application or applications to support and that's what they do. They are associated with service management, and they will fix things whether they're infrastructure or software or both. Depending on the make-up of the team and its capacity they also could pick up some small projects and improvements. Thus, we had the fledgling concept of DevOps in operation some 35 years ago.

Somewhere along the line, the ops part has certainly taken off and as any number of toolsets and applications which operational people can use along with infrastructure side of things toys for the boys, I term this, although increasingly not always boys. The development side seems to have been pushed out completely which is quite a sad thing to see because of the huge potential for the original concept of DevOps. It has seen a revival in the forum of product teams which surprise surprise, is developers and operational support working together to deliver support and projects, it only took them thirty years to do what we were doing but I will give them credit for giving it a different name.

When product or project teams start delivering, they will have a requirement on operations and support to do certain things for them like open firewalls. These kinds of requests will not be a one-off big bang, but they're going to be consistent and low level through the duration of the delivery. I think I've mentioned enough about budgets so far but the concept that somebody is going to turn around and say I need two days of a network person's time and I'm going to spend, money and effort in the organisation to raise resource requests, raise budget codes and all the other financial wastage which is associated with these small requests is not in any way worthwhile in terms of cost or in the inordinate overhead terms of time that it wastes within organisations. Get used to the idea that you will have a constant low-level requirement to supply staff and services to Agile projects. Depending on the size of the project you may wish to dedicate a person full-time to it. I would probably expect that this is the exception, and this will only be very large projects that it will be necessary for, but it can happen. A more realistic model is one where you take a reasonable estimate of the amount of time from your team that will require from projects. This will be an individual call, but you need to decide whether that level of commitment can be supplied from the existing team or whether you need to increase the headcount. The business knows that it has a call on the network team to do things that are going to happen regardless of the paperwork let's do it in the manner which causes the least friction and causes the least pain. I have a resource pool available for projects. The project manager comes along and wishes to access that resource pool. You can ask if the said project manager has a budget to pay for his little slice of the resource pool and if you confirm it then it is just a matter of agreeing on the timing. The network engineer then allocates his portion of his week to that particular budget. More importantly, things get done and the finance department will also be happy because the budget code is getting used. So realistically if you're going to have to support projects you need to have the headcount to support projects and the projects can call off against the headcount and chargeback to the project codes. The project manager gets access to the resources without extraordinary amounts of pain.

You will need to discuss this with the Human Resources department. There is no point being Ostrich type organisation pretending that the projects that we just authorised for this financial year will magically resource themselves. Or give the project managers and department heads a headache when they need people for the team, OK let's just solve the problem at three times the cost and hire in contractors. Guess what this is not a one-off, believe it or not, we do more than one project a year and for some organisations, they even do projects in the next year. Why all the surprise. It should be possible to look back over the last two years because we have all those lovely budget codes and say on average, we have 30 % of our staff allocating time to some project. Half are internal, and half are contracts. So, I am short of 15% of the headcount which we backfill with contractors. As the contractors are normally three times more expensive, we are racking up 45% of the entire resource budget spent by the organisation to supply 15%

of your staff needs. It is not going to take a genius to see that is not a great use of money. You will always need some specialists for the short term.

Now ask yourself what the headcount would look like if we only wanted 5% to be contractors. Start dealing with reality and get the people you need. This absolute waste of time on pretending to keep the headcount down when the facts prove otherwise. As an organisation, we are lying to ourselves the only happy people are the HR department because they are trying to keep to a concept that was introduced in 1972 and now forms part of KPIs for most HR departments, without anyone asking if just possibly anything has changed in the labour market since 1972, and wither that is a good KPI for us to be looking at headcount, above the pain to business, late deliveries, additional admin and exorbitant cost to the business. If you want to prove it, ask the HR department how many employees we have, then check the number of user accounts you have. Where did all those extra accounts magically appear from and who is paying for them!

The principal is ok if we keep our headcount to the minimum required to do the job. Then we will be "frugal" with our spending. I am ok with that, but the key part of that sentence is the minimum required. When we set the minimum required 20-30% below what we need and backfill with very expensive resources, can you explain to me how that makes things better? Let me give you an example, you are running a café seven days a week and decide to hire a cook only for five days a week to keep costs under control. Now we have a shortfall and need someone to cover the weekends. Ah, we have a solution, let's hire a Michelin Chef two days a week at $500 per day and congratulate ourselves on the fact that we have kept the headcount down. If you don't think that is a good model, why are we so keen to embrace it in organisations. I am all for not employing people you don't need but please explain to me the reasoning behind not employing people you do need and replacing that shortfall at triple the price and explain how that helps with good financial controls?

When we have a product team who not only implements the projects but also is responsible for the maintenance and support of the product then we do have somewhere to go. The headcount should include a percentage for project work. I had an example of a team like this where 25% was budgeted for routine maintenance like back-ups, patching and security things. Another 35% was dedicated to handling support calls and the final 40% was for projects and enhancements. Each activity had its pot (budget code) and at the end of the week, the code was filled in on a timesheet. If things changed from year to year, we could tweak the proportion. If we had server operating system upgrades one year we would cut back on the available project allocation. This worked just fine, could be flexible and Finance were ok with it as long as the percentages roughly added up by the end of the financial year. If project requirements were high one year, we would have to put some of the upgrades of maintenance tasks on life support but we knew that we would get that time back when the project pressure was a little lower.

This is a really good model to adopt. It ticks all the boxes and when a project manager came along and asked, we would like to add some pages to the site, the reply was "what do you need and when do you want us to start", It was an Agile product team, so it could deal flexibly with things. The project request is added to the backlog and according to the priority, the business gives it can be picked up in the next sprint.

There was a nice story that illustrated this. On a Tuesday a Project Manager appeared with a data problem they were having. They Outlined what it was and how they would like to mine the data and have it presented. This was causing big problems and an ISO audit coming up in a few weeks could fail if we could not get the data in the right format. We asked for a business contact and checked with them the fine details. The following Friday I invited the PM and the business contact to a meeting. They assumed that we were there to discuss requirements and scoping documents, fill in forms and discuss budget codes. To their utter surprise, it was a demo of the web page with the report. After a bit of discussion, it transpired that it was great, but could we move one of the columns two to the left and could they get it filtered by region. OK was my reply see you next Friday for another demo.

I am sure most of you that have approached an operational team to do something for you, have had just this lovely experience and were delighted at the speed and ease with which things are done, NOT... However, it can be this easy. The team can handle project and enhancement work baked in. It was only a matter of prioritizing what work when.

I will be reasonable and highlight a few cases where we may need external project staff. They tend to fall into time-boxed one-off events like acquisitions and mergers, or it could be replacing all the PCs and Laptops with a new operating system. These kinds of things are big hitters on resources but will only last a matter of months. So, for these kinds of things, may need contractors. Also, if we are doing something new then we may need to bring in expertise. I as an Agile Coach has done just such tasks many times introducing Agile then running through one or two deliveries, then off to the next organisation to do it all over again. I completely understand that we will need some contractors, I would suggest that somewhere between 5-10% should be where you want to aim for.

The reality for most businesses they will have a series of initiatives, upgrades and new product lines. Just look back when we discuss departmental budgets there are always things people want to do, they just do not always get them funded. It is more realistic to consider there is going to be a level of project activity between 10-25% of your staffing profile. Find out what it is and demand that we stop the headcount nonsense and hire the level of staff to do operations and projects.

Be warned I have talked about how people don't like change, but there is a headcount problem for HR. If we are not hiring in all those temporary contractors, the workload on HR is going to drop and that may mean they have a headcount that is too high. I have on occasions pondered what the protocols are for HR to make HR redundant? It is workload and change so you will get push back, but start asking questions like what was the cost of contractors last year and what was that as a proportion of our operational staff budget. Don't let them add in very high paid VPS as they aren't involved in the day to day projects. Keep it on the shop floor so you measure like for like. When you see the figures, I bet they will back down as they will not be able to justify the cost.

I would suggest further that we have our normal operational load and also our normal project and initiatives load. Add the two together and that is what your headcount should be. If this is done there should never be a case in normal operations that some part of the support organisation turns around and says we don't have enough people to support this. It may be the case that it has been a merger or acquisition and suddenly additional work has been thrust upon you, but I suspect that most organisations have a low-level requirement for project work year after year and instead of that being problem the blocks projects gives you grief and everybody else why not get your act together and put in a headcount which meets the real requirements which include project work. By the time a project comes along and says we need somebody it is too late, as support organisations are great at asking for money to develop the latest new technologies, we are sadly lacking in using some of that technology to spot the bleeding obvious that every organisation has projects, and those projects need people so resource them.

Human Resources

The ideal position is that you take existing staff and combine them into teams that manage the technical side of supporting and updating a product. The product normally will encompass a bit of software or a service like an email or the HR system. In principle, this is relatively easy. Just like setting up a small department or a regional office. Where the complexity comes in for human resource teams is the change in traditional managerial hierarchy. Agile teams generally do not have a defined line manager. The team delivers as a whole and there is a great deal of time spent by the Scrum Master breaking down traditional structures.

Like a sports team each member has his or her role to play but no one is the boss within the team. It is done by agreement within the team that the task is ready to work on. The Product Owner and the Business have agreed the task is important enough to include in the next sprint. This sprint will last between two to four weeks and at the end of it the results of the task will be demonstrated to the business and if they agree the new functionality or feature works as expected then it will go live. Repeat this process for the next sprint and so on.

What the observant will have noticed is there is no manager here telling the team what to do, the teams are focused on the delivery of the product and not part of the larger department for testers or analysts. They are not seconded or borrowed from their home department, they move lock stock and barrel to the Agile product team. They are fully dedicated to product delivery, in a similar way to how many people are assigned to a project. The only difference is that they will not be back in their department in a few months when the project is complete. Rather think of the product team as a new department and the staff are moving permanently to this department. With Agile teams often the only contact that they have with their former line managers is for approval of holidays and of course the complete farce of a line manager doing an appraisal on a staff member, that they have no idea what they have been doing, and the last time they saw them was the Christmas party. When a staff member joins the team they leave their old department, The previous line manager is no longer relevant, and the link should be removed. If you really really have to designate someone then put down the Scrum Master or Product Owner but this should be seen as purely admin and not a position of authority.

I touched on this before in the testing section, and it may have crossed your mind we have team leaders, managers and department heads in development, testing and analysts to name but a few. What will they do for the business if all the previous staff members that used to report to them are away working in Agile teams? They don't have anyone left to manage or be a team leader too. In some organisations, this effectively redundant management layer is redirected to quality assurance roles or research and development on what tooling the teams should be using. This transfers the role from direct line management to one of facilitating the teams. In other organisations, they are just seen as now redundant, and they are let go. The onus is on the previous line managers to justify to someone with a budget that they can still deliver some value to the business.

All of this can be considered admin and has nothing to do with delivering good quality software. How the HR department wants to handle it is up to them. Please do not try and organise teams to suit your software or budget codes. People should not be forced to work inefficiently. Equally, we do not want to have entries in software systems that are complete fiction just because something is a required field on a screen, if your software does not support Agile then it is no longer fit for purpose and should be changed.

Possibly you need your own Agile product team to look after the HR system.

The next area to be addressed is the dreaded appraisal process. It has become a common practice throughout the year to do some sort of assessment on individuals. I have never been able to get a satisfactory answer to a fundamental question I have about this process. If we recognise the value of teams and cooperation, why then do we measure the individual and not the team. Many Agile focused organisations address this by giving team goals and targets. The team delivers or it does not. Therefore, the whole team gets rewarded or punished as appropriate the focus on the individual's measurement is removed.

The traditional progression up the corporate ladder. We have just removed the team leader, team managers and department heads because they are no longer needed. So where do you go if the roles that you may have wanted to apply for no longer exist? We want people that will support and deliver change to software products for the next five years, there is nowhere to progress to, you can only get better at what you are doing and improve the process to make your life easier. This needs to be considered as part of the recruitment process. We do not need highflyers, what we are looking for is the willingness to change, adapt to problem solving and technical competence. We want people who are good at their job. They are not going anywhere and need to accept that. Some organisations will rotate some people around the teams a bit like the army does, after two years your tour of duty is done, and you can move to another team. While this is possible, it is not compulsory. When you apply for a job as a bus driver you can reasonably expect that you will be a bus driver in three or five years. This also applies to our Agile product teams, if you are recruited to support and apply the change to the HR system then that is your job.

It assumed that much of the productivity we will gain is from having the team stay together and gain product knowledge. We get 100-150% on top of what basic Agile offers by keeping people together. For the business, this productivity gain is too large to ignore.

We assume that this team will also deliver traditional project deliveries therefore the size of the team needs to accommodate this. It may be common to say 50% on maintenance and support and the other 50% is available for project type deliveries. The adage here is that we bring work to the teams not the teams to work, the best people to deliver any change are the people that manage the system on a day to day basis and know it inside out.

In a misconceived assumption that keeping the head count down is a good thing, we pare down the support teams to the bare minimum so there is no headroom to take on the project work. No problem we can hire contractors or outsource the work at three or four times the cost. We will spend a small fortune kicking off a project and hiring expensive day rate staff. These new people will, of course, know nothing about our system and will spend three months bugging the existing support teams for information, IT departments need to be mobilised to create accounts and supply equipment for these staff and then do it in reverse in six or twelve months when it is all over. We claim that we have held the FTE count while costing the business huge amounts of cash. An alternative to all of this is to realise especially in this age where software is expected to be continually updated and kept up to date with all the latest security fixes.

Recognise that we deliver change, sometimes we call it a project, but the name is of no importance. Figure out what percentage of the team's effort needs to be expended on change and resource it upfront. Stop the day rate revolving door and just hire the staff that is needed and keep the benefits of the knowledge capital within the business. I have done the forensic cost accounting on this. Over five years the cost is plus or minus 10% compared to kicking off projects. Most projects eat up 10-20% just to run the project. Do the maths 1.5 years of a contractor normally equals 4 to 5 years for an employee cost.

We may also want to look at the supporting parts of the business which includes finance, payroll, project management office and not to forget the HR department itself. When we bring project work to our adequately resourced teams, we do not have this mad dash to hire people, the reporting is simplified, costs are more or less fixed costs because our teams are stable and fixed. There are a lot of people that will no longer be needed. This will have a hit on HR in year one. Hiring people to resize the teams to be able to handle projects and making redundant the managers and excess admin support staff that are no longer needed. After year one it should settle down and then it is time to turn your attention to what the appropriate size of the HR department should be.

Training

There may be times when we need to do a big training program traditionally. This could be when we swap out the HR or payroll system. Everyone needs to be trained from the login screen up. If you are organisation is geographically distributed, you will be on the road for a while delivering the training. Alternatively, when we do Waterfall, it comes in big lumps of functionality and again needs this traditional training model. Time to get the passport out again.

In Agile deliveries, we do not have big bangs. There will be small incremental changes every two to four weeks. The changes are small. There is a new menu item, and some process now sends an email confirmation to the user. In another 4 weeks, we will have a new report, in another two weeks we will have the ability to email a report in PDF format from within the app.

Here is the problem. There is no point waiting until there are enough changes to justify flying to Florida. People are using the app and need to know how the new changes work, but no one is going to justify the cost of your flight and hotel to Florida, to tell staff that there is a new button to email a report, now are they?

The most common answer is we develop videos and micro training to support each release. You will pick up new animation or video skills to lay out what the small changes are. This will normally be done in the office and not involve travel.

This brings us to the people problem. If you are good at standing in a classroom being a teacher, you may not have the desire or skill set to want to become an animator or video editor, voice-over person or such skill set.

The result is that several of your existing trainers will walk and look for more traditional jobs while they are still available.

If you are in the HR department then be prepared for this a good chunk of your human capital is about to walk out the door. This should not be the end of the world because if they walk it is probably down to the fact that they do not have or do not want to change their skill set and would have not been much good at the new job anyway.

The Wrong Key Performance Indicators

In the previous chapters, we covered off the reality that managers care about visible things. This for them is a Key Performance Indicator or KPI. There often gets distortion in the workplace or the markets when we focus minds on the key. We saw this in the extreme with the banking collapse through subprime mortgages in 2008. It should be no surprise that if you make a large part of a person's remuneration based on the number of mortgages they sell, they will then find a new and wonderful way to sell more mortgages.

If we consider more business-related KPI, let's ask the question if they distort our market?

HeadCount.

The aim is to keep the headcount or staffing profile at a set level and be seen as a well-performing Human Resources department.

Possible Result.

We hire contractors at three or four times the price, then pretend that they do not exist on our books for headcount even if they have been sitting in the same chair contracting for the last five years.

Support Service Level Agreements

Aim to return service to an operational state or supply a service within an agreed timescale

Possible Result

Staff are told it takes 10 days to get a user account set up and 20 days to get a laptop and think you are having a laugh. When they see you are serious, they walk away muttering things I cannot put in this book, and we wonder why the IT department gets a bad rep. The possibility of us hiring someone was such a farfetched outlandish possibility that we could not possibly have a laptop sitting in a cupboard ready to go. That would be wasteful, far better to have a contractor at $650 per day sitting around reading the instructions for the coffee machine rather than doing some work.

Annual Survey

Obtain feedback from staff, identify areas of improvement.

My Result.

I will save you the money every staff survey returns the same thing. Management doesn't understand the pressure we work under. Our department is wonderful, and we could cure cancer and solve climate change ourselves if it was not for all the other departments. There you go just saved you £20K

Annual Budgets

When we allocate funds for the year ahead to maintain service or incorporate some new process or feature requested by the business or external market or legal requirement.

Possible Result

Predicting things more than thirty days out is difficult and ninety days is about your limit before you may as well throw some dice. Predicting the future is not easy, if it was, we would all be millionaires and living in mansions.

You are restricting the business to a process that is not based in reality and for the sake of the Finance department based on reporting to the taxman. This has nothing to do with what and how the business operates or serves its customers unless your business is doing tax returns. You would not arrange your holiday around when your groceries supplier wants to prepare the shop for Christmas. That is their business and we as the business should not be restricted by when the financial year-end is. Our customers do not care why should you. A more realistic option would be quarterly budget allocations, giving stage gates to performance and preventing dead money from being allocated to things that will never happen.

These are just some examples, but I am sure if you look at what KPI you have and not mission statements, you may find some that generate bad behaviour.

Desire Vs Outcome

Not all are black and white. The ServiceDesk is a good example. Say you think the 10 minutes on each support call is too long. You raise a KPI to say no more than six minutes then wrap up the call.

Possible Result

Second-line support complains that they are getting a lot more tasks than they used to. The customer now finds that instead of the ServiceDesk doing some tasks for them, they are directed to a website and the customer experience is lowered.

The study of Economics talks about opportunity costs. If you spend $5 on a hotdog you no longer have that $5 to buy a magazine. In this example, the opportunity cost is the magazine that you can no longer buy. Think of what the opportunity cost is for each KPI you want to introduce and whether the opportunity cost is something we want to promote. Again, with the ServiceDesk, I see lots of statistics about the number of calls, call duration and fix rate. I am yet to see a stat on how many problems causing the calls to get fixed.

Possible Negative effects

To quote an ex CEO of Google...

Social Media companies want to maximise profits.

The way to maximise profits is by increasing user engagement

The most effective way to inspire engagement is to invoke outrage.

Thus, we see a KPI that could potentially have social harm. There is an opportunity cost to every action, try and think what the unintended consequences of your KPI could be. It may just not be something you want to encourage.

The Process In Numbers

Here are your takeaway headlines

Introducing basic Agile teams improves productivity 25-50%

When teams are formed and are self-organised, they no longer need team leaders, managers, heads of departments in the traditional roles. 30-80% of these roles can go

Agile teams reduce rework and testing by 30%

The number of Admin staff is reduced with simpler reporting and fixed cost model. 10-30% of Finance, PMO and change management roles are now redundant

Teams that work together get better at it over time do not be surprised to see a 100% productivity increase in the first year.

If you produce software in half the time, then you can produce twice as much or half the staff. Your call after year one.

Software defects are normally reduced by at least 200%

If you want to argue your organisation should not adopt Agile you need to explain why the above is not good for the business.

Thanks for your Time

Regards

A

The legal stuff

A Business Managers Guide To Agile
A Handbook For Transforming The Workplace And Job Roles

By Andy.S.Evans

Published by YE&EE Publishing

ISBN 9798799183769

Printed in Great Britain
by Amazon